KOREAN

Speak Korean With Confidence

Compiled by
Soyeung Koh & Gene Baik

TUTTLE Publishing
Tokyo | Rutland, Vermont | Singapore

The Tuttle Story: "Books to Span the East and West"

Most people are surprised to learn that the world's largest publisher of books on Asia had its humble beginnings in the tiny American state of Vermont. The company's founder, Charles E. Tuttle, belonged to a New England family steeped in publishing. And his first love was naturally books—especially old and rare editions.

Immediately after WW II, serving in Tokyo under General Douglas MacArthur, Tuttle was tasked with reviving the Japanese publishing industry. He later founded the Charles E. Tuttle Publishing Company, which thrives today as one of the world's leading independent publishers.

Though a westerner, Tuttle was hugely instrumental in bringing a knowledge of Japan and Asia to a world hungry for information about the East. By the time of his death in 1993, Tuttle had published over 6,000 books on Asian culture, history and art—a legacy honored by the Japanese emperor with the "Order of the Sacred Treasure," the highest tribute Japan can bestow upon a non-Japanese.

With a backlist of 1,500 titles, Tuttle Publishing is more active today than at any time in its past—inspired by Charles Tuttle's core mission to publish fine books to span the East and West and provide a greater understanding of each.

Published by Tuttle Publishing, an imprint of Periplus Editions (HK) Ltd.

www.tuttlepublishing.com

Copyright © 2012 Periplus Editions (HK) Ltd

ISBN: 978-0-8048-4241-9

First edition
19 18 17 16 15 14 13 12
11 10 9 8 7 6 5 4 3 2   1209MP

Printed in Singapore

TUTTLE PUBLISHING® is a registered trademark of Tuttle Publishing, a division of Periplus Editions (HK) Ltd.

Distributed by
North America, Latin America & Europe
Tuttle Publishing
364 Innovation Drive
North Clarendon, VT 05759-9436 U.S.A.
Tel: 1 (802) 773-8930; Fax: 1 (802) 773-6993
info@tuttlepublishing.com
www.tuttlepublishing.com

Japan
Tuttle Publishing
Yaekari Building, 3rd Floor, 5-4-12 Osaki
Shinagawa-ku, Tokyo 141 0032
Tel: (81) 3 5437-0171; Fax: (81) 3 5437-0755
sales@tuttle.co.jp   www.tuttle.co.jp

Asia Pacific
Berkeley Books Pte. Ltd.
61 Tai Seng Avenue #02-12, Singapore 534167
Tel: (65) 6280-1330; Fax: (65) 6280-6290
inquiries@periplus.com.sg   www.periplus.com

Indonesia
PT Java Books Indonesia
Jl. Rawa Gelam IV No. 9
Kawasan Industri Pulogadung
Jakarta 13930, Indonesia
Tel: 62 (21) 4682 1088; Fax: 62 (21) 461 0206
crm@periplus.co.id   www.periplus.com

Contents

Introduction

● ●

● **Welcome to the Tuttle Essential Language series, covering all of the most popular world languages. These books are basic guides in communicating in the language. They're concise, accessible and easy to understand, and you'll find them indispensable on your trip abroad to get you where you want to go, pay the right prices and do everything you've been planning to do.**

Each guide is divided into 15 themed sections and starts with a pronunciation table which explains the phonetic pronunciation to all the words and sentences you'll need to know, and a grammar guide which will help you construct basic sentences in your chosen language. The back of the book presents an extensive word list.

Throughout the book you'll come across boxes with a 🔊 beside them. These are designed to help you if you can't understand what your listener is saying to you. Hand the book over to them and encourage them to point to the appropriate answer to the question you are asking.

Other boxes in the book—this time without the symbol—give alphabetical listings of themed words with their English translations beside them.

For extra clarity, we have put all phonetic pronunciations of the foreign language terms in bold.

This book covers all subjects you are likely to come across during the course of a visit, from reserving a room for the night to ordering food and drink at a restaurant and what to do if your car breaks down or you lose your traveler's checks and money. With over 2,000 commonly used words and essential sentences at your fingertips you can rest assured that you will be able to get by in all situations, so let *Essential Korean* become your passport to learning to speak with confidence!

Pronunciation guide

Transcriptions

Korean words and expressions in this book are romanized using the Revised Romanization of Korean prepared and authorized by the Korean Government (see below). Along with the principles of this system, some transcription conventions are adopted as follows:

(a) Words are romanized according to sound rather than to Korean spelling. However, in the case of verbs in the glossary section, the transcription of tensed sounds has been minimized so that the user can identify and utilize the verb stem without much confusion (e.g. to be = **itda**, instead of **itta**).

(b) Where there is an expression consisting of more than one word, a space is given to mark the word boundary.

(c) Where necessary, a dot (.) is used to mark the syllable boundary so that confusion in pronunciation can be avoided.

(d) Three dots (...) are used in a grammatical phrase where a noun is required.

(e) In the glossary index, a hyphen (-) is used to indicate a verb stem or the optional adjective form derived from an adjectival verb.

(f) In the glossary index, for descriptive words, both adjectival verb forms (e.g. to be pretty = **yeppeuda**) and adjective forms (e.g. pretty = **yeppeun**) are given.

The Korean alphabet and its romanization

1) **Consonants**
   (a) **Simple consonants**

ㄱ g, k	ㄴ n	ㄷ d, t	ㄹ r, l	ㅁ m
ㅂ b, p	ㅅ s	ㅇ ng	ㅈ j	ㅊ ch
ㅋ k	ㅌ t	ㅍ p	ㅎ h	

   (b) **Double consonants**

ㄲ kk	ㄸ tt	ㅃ pp	ㅆ ss	ㅉ jj

2) Vowels

(a) Simple vowels

ㅏ	a	ㅓ	eo	ㅗ	o	ㅜ	u	ㅡ eu
ㅣ	i	ㅐ	ae	ㅔ	e	ㅚ	oe	ㅟ wi

ㅏ **a**   ㅓ **eo**   ㅗ **o**   ㅜ **u**   ㅡ **eu**
ㅣ **i**   ㅐ **ae**   ㅔ **e**   ㅚ **oe**   ㅟ **wi**

(b) Compound vowels

ㅑ **ya**   ㅕ **yeo**   ㅛ **yo**   ㅠ **yu**   ㅒ **yae**
ㅖ **ye**   ㅘ **wa**   ㅙ **wae**   ㅝ **wo**   ㅞ **we**
ㅢ **ui**

Reading romanized Korean

There is a very important distinction between the reading of romanized Korean and English. The Korean romanization system depicts the sound of Korean in English letters to help foreigners communicate in Korean. Because English letters used in romanized Korean are sound symbols, they have to be pronounced in a certain way only. They should not be treated as those in English words. In English words, the sound value assigned to a certain letter varies according to different words. For example, 'a' in *apple, father, syllable* and *date* all have different sound values. Unless you have learnt the English phonetic symbols, you might read romanized Korean 'a' differently from the expected sound depending on what romanized Korean words you have. For example, you might read a as 'a' in *apple* when you get the romanized Korean word **sam** (삼) 'three'; or you might read it as 'a' in *syllable* for either 'a' in the romanized Korean word **saram** (사람) 'person', etc.

To avoid this type of confusion, some examples of English words containing sounds equivalent to some of the romanized Korean vowels and consonants are given as follows (approximate guideline only):

Vowels: eo, **eu**, **ae** and **oe** are single vowels in romanized Korean as shown below. Therefore careful attention should be given to these vowels in not splitting them into two. Also, careful attention should be given to **u** [우] not to be read as English 'you'. Some common vowels which might confuse you are:

a	아	**ah**, f**a**ther	(but shorter)
eo	어	b**ir**d, s**er**ve	
o	오	b**a**ll, p**o**re	(but shorter)
u	우	sh**oe**, sch**oo**l	(but shorter)
eu	으	br**o**ken, g**o**lden	

i	이	b**ee**, sh**ee**p	(but shorter)
ae	애	**a**pple, b**a**d	
e	에	b**e**d, **e**gg	
oe	외	w**e**t, w**e**lcome	

Consonants: There won't be much trouble in pronouncing romanized Korean consonants except some tensed ones which require a relatively strong muscular effort in the vocal organs without the expulsion of air. Some examples are given as follow:

kk	ㄲ	s**k**i, s**k**y	(**k** after **s**)
tt	ㄸ	s**t**eak, s**t**ing	(**t** after **s**)
pp	ㅃ	s**p**eak, s**p**y	(**p** after **s**)
ss	ㅆ	**s**ea, **s**ir	(**s** before a vowel)
jj	ㅉ	bri**dg**e, mi**dg**et	(similar to a tutting sound in an exhaling way)

Basic grammar

1 Word order

Unlike in English, the Korean verb (action verb or adjectival verb) comes at the end of a sentence or clause. Also the Korean word order is quite flexible because there are special markers attached to the words in a sentence. They are called particles, and they mark the function of the words in a sentence: which word is a subject or an object etc. By contrast, in English you cannot simply change the word order in a sentence without violating its meaning because the position of words in a sentence tells us which is a subject or an object. For example, two different sentences, 'The cat chased a mouse' and 'A mouse chased the cat' have the same meaning in Korean because of the particles affixed to the subject and the object respectively. 'The cat-**ga** a mouse-**reul** chased' and 'A mouse-**reul** the cat-**ga** chased' (**ga** indicates 'the cat' is a subject, **reul** indicates 'a mouse' is an object).

2 Common participle

Some of the common particles are:

Subject marker: **i** (이) (after a word ending in a consonant), **ga** (가) (after a word ending in a vowel);

Topic/contrast marker: **eun** (은) (after a word ending in a consonant), **neun** (는) (after a word ending in a vowel);

Object marker: **eul** (을) (after a word ending in a consonant), **reul** (를) (after a word ending in a vowel);

Place/time marker (in/at/on) : **e** (에) (a place marker **eseo** (에서) has a special usage but it is not covered here)

3 Subject omission

Although the subject comes at the beginning of the sentence, it is often omitted if it is clearly understood from the context by the participants in a conversation.

Where do you live?	**eodi saseyo?**	(where live?)
I live in Sydney	**sidenie sarayo**	(Sydney live)
What are you doing?	**mwo haeyo?**	(what do?)
I am studying	**gongbuhaeyo**	(study)

4 Action verb and adjectival verb

Korean adjectives conjugate like verbs, therefore they are often called adjectival verbs or descriptive verbs. To distinguish a normal verb from an adjectival verb or a descriptive verb, a normal verb is called an action verb. You can see most of the adjectives in the glossary section of this book have two entries, one in a dictionary form which ends in **-da** (다) and the other in an adjectival form which modifies a noun in front of it. Verb conjugation is carried out by adding infixes or suffixes to the verb stem. The verb stem is the part of the verb remaining after **-da** (다) is taken away from the dictionary form of the verb.

5 Honorific language

When you speak Korean, you have to know who you are talking to. Depending on your relationship with them, their age and their social status, you have to choose an appropriate level of politeness when you talk. There are several speech levels in Korean. These speech levels are indicated in a sentence by the sentence-final suffixes attached to the end of verb stems. We will not cover all these levels here. We will only talk about the most common polite endings, which travelers are most likely to use in a real situation: formal polite form, informal polite form and informal honorific form.

Formal polite form

This is used in formal situations, and is common in men's conversation. You add **-mnida** (ㅂ니다) if the verb stem ends in a vowel. Otherwise, you add **-seumnida** (습니다). If you want to make a question sentence, you simply change the final **-da** (다) of these formal polite verb-endings into **kka**? (까?).

Informal polite form

This is common in daily conversation, and is especially used by women. This form requires a bit more complicated process compared to the others. Firstly you have to look at the final vowel of the verb stem. If it is **a** (아) or **o** (오), you add **-ayo** (아요). Otherwise you add **-eoyo** (어요). If the verb stem ends in a vowel, you come to have two consecutive vowels after this conjugation. Two consecutive vowels are usually required to be fused into one. For example, **o** (오) and **a** (아) become **wa** (와). If the two consecutive vowels are the same vowel, one of them will be eliminated. If the verb stem ends in **eu** (으), which is the weakest vowel in Korean, it will also be eliminated.

There are a couple of exceptions to this conjugation rule. If the verb stem ends in **ha** (하), you always change this **ha** (하) into **haeyo** (해요). For the verb **ida** (이다) (to be: equation), you change this particular verb into **yeyo** (예요) after a word ending in a vowel. Otherwise you change this into **ieyo** (이에요). To make a question sentence, you simply say the same sentence with a rising tone at the end as you normally do in a question. There is no grammatical change between a statement and a question sentence in this level of language.

Informal honorific form

When you talk to the people clearly superior to you, such as your clients or guests, much older people or socially high-ranking people, you use an honorific form of language to show your respect to them. Of course you never use this form to refer to yourself. The process of this conjugation is quite simple. You add **-seyo** (세요) if the verb stem ends in a vowel. Otherwise, you add **-euseyo** (으세요).

Too many levels to work out which one to use? Don't panic! They are all polite forms at least. Whichever form you use, you are still in the range of common expectation from the native Korean speakers. Anyway, they often use a mixture of all these levels of language even in a conversation with the same person.

6 Some useful grammatical items

The following grammatical items might help you to make new sentences as long as you know the words.

Would/Could you do something for me?

(jom)   verb stem   +   a/eo jusigesseoyo?
(좀)   verb stem   +   아/어 주시겠어요?

If the final vowel in the verb stem is **a** (아) or **o** (오), you choose **-a** (아). Otherwise you choose **-eo** (어). Please refer to the section on 'informal polite form' for more details on how to add **-a/eo** (-아/어), how to deal with consecutive vowels and the exception of **ha** (하) etc.

to fix, 고치다, gochida	...jom gochyeo jusigesseoyo?	Could you fix ...?
to find, 찾다, chatda	...jom chaja jusigesseoyo?	Could you find ...?
to see, 보다, boda	...jom bwa jusigesseoyo?	Could you see ...?

Please do something (for me)

(jom)   verb stem   +   **a/eo juseyo?**

(좀)   verb stem   +   아/어 주세요?

Please refer to the above to see how you add **-a** (아) or **-o** (오).

to fix, 고치다, gochida	...jom gochyeo juseyo?	Please fix ...
to write down, 쓰다, **sseuda**	...jom sseo juseyo?	Please write ...down
to see, 보다, **boda**	...jom bwa juseyo?	Please see ...

Don't do it, please

verb stem   +   **ji maseyo**

verb stem   +   지 마세요

to eat, 먹다, **meokda**	...meokji maseyo	Don't eat ..., please
to smoke, 담배 피우다, **dambae piuda**	**dambae piuji maseyo**	Don't smoke, please
to come, 오다, **oda**	**oji maseyo**	Don't come, please

I want to do something

verb stem   +   **go sipeoyo**

verb stem   +   고 싶어요

to go, 가다, **gada**	**gago sipeoyo**	I want to go
to see, 보다, **boda**	...-reul/eul bogo sipeoyo	I want to see ...
to buy, 사다, **sada**	...-reul/eul sago sipeoyo	I want to buy ...

1 The Basics

1. The Basics

 Personal details

surname	성 seong
first name	이름 i reum
initials	이닛샬 i nit syal
address (street/number)	주소 (가/번지) ju so (ga/beon ji)
postal code/town	우편번호/시 u pyeon-beon ho/si
sex (male/female)	성 (남성/여성) seong (nam seong/yeo seong)
nationality	국적 guk jeok
date of birth	생년월일 saeng nyeo nwo ril
place of birth	출생지 chul saeng ji
occupation	직업 ji geop
marital status	결혼 여부 gyeol hon-yeo bu
married/single	기혼/미혼 gi hon/mi hon
widowed	사별한 sa byeol han
(number of) children	자녀(수) ja nyeo(su)
place and date of issue	발행 기관 및 일자 bal haeng gi gwan mit il jja

passport/identity card/ driving license number	여권/신분증/운전면허 번호 yeo kkwon/sin bun jjeung/ un jeon myeon heo beon ho
signature	서명 seo.myeong

1.2 Today or tomorrow?

What day is it today?	오늘은 무슨 요일이에요? O neu reun mu seun yo i ri e yo?
Today's Monday	오늘은 월요일이에요 O neu reun wo ryo i r-i e yo
- Tuesday	화요일이에요 hwa yo i r-i e yo
- Wednesday	수요일이에요 su yo i r i e yo
- Thursday	목요일이에요 mo gyo i r-i e yo
- Friday	금요일이에요 geu myo i r-i e yo
- Saturday	토요일이에요 to yo i r-i e yo
- Sunday	일요일이에요 i ryo i r-i e yo
in January	일월에 i rwo re
since February	이월부터 i wo bu teo
in spring	봄에 bo me
in summer	여름에 yeo reu me
in autumn	가을에 ga eu re
in winter	겨울에 gyeo u re

2011	이천십일 년 **I cheon si bil lyeon**
the twentieth century	이십 세기 **i sip se gi**
the twenty-first century	이십일 세기 **i si bil se gi**
What's the date today?	오늘이 몇 일이에요? **O neu ri myeo chi ri e yo?**
Today's the 24th	오늘은 이십 사일이에요 **O neu reun i sip sa i ri e yo**
Monday 3 November	십일월 삼일, 월요일이에요 **Si bi rwol sa mil, wo ryo i ri e yo**
in the morning	아침에 **a chi me**
in the afternoon	오후에 **o hu e**
in the evening	저녁에 **jeo nyeo ge**
at night	밤에 **ba me**
this morning	오늘 아침 **o neul a chim**
this afternoon	오늘 오후 **o neul ohu**
this evening	오늘 저녁 **o neul-jyeo nyeok**
tonight	오늘 밤 **o neul bam**
last night	어제 밤 **eo jet bam**
this week	이번 주 **i beon ju**
next month	다음 달 **da eum dal**
last year	작년 **jang nyeon**

next...	...다음 **...da-eum**
in...days/weeks/months/ years	...일/주/달/년 후에 **...il/ju/dal/nyeon hu e**
...weeks ago	... 주 전
day off	비번, 쉬는 날 **bi beon, swi neun nal**

1.3 What time is it?

What time is it?	지금 몇 시예요? **Ji geum myeot-si ye yo?**
It's nine o'clock	아홉시에요 **A hop si e yo**
- five past ten	열시 오분이에요 **yeol si o bu ni e yo**
- a quarter past eleven	열한시 십오분이에요 **yeol han si si bo bu ni e yo**
- twenty past twelve	열두시 이 십 분이에요 **yeol du si i sip bun i e yo**
- half past one	한시 반 이에요 **han si ba ni e yo**
- twenty-five to three	세시 이 십오분 전이에요 **se si i si bo bun jeo ni e yo**
- a quarter to four	네시 십오분 전이에요 **ne si si bo bun jeo ni e yo**
- ten to five	다섯시 십분 전이에요 **da seot si sip bun jeo ni e yo**
It's midday (twelve noon)	정오(낮 열 두시)에요 **Jeong-o(nat yeol du si)-e yo**
It's midnight	자정(밤 열 두시)이에요 **Ja jeong(bam yeol du si)-i e yo**
half an hour	삼 십 분 **sam sip bun**
What time?	몇 시예요? **Myeot si ye yo?**

What time can I come by?	몇 시에 가면 돼요? Myeot si e ga myeon dwae yo?
At...	...에 ...e
After...	...후에 ...hu e
Before...	...전에 ...jeo ne
Between...and...(o'clock)	...시에서...시 사이에 ...si e seo...si sa i e
From...to...	...부터...까지 ...bu teo...kka ji
In...minutes	...분 후에 ...bun hu e
- an hour	한시간 후에 han si gan hu e
-...hours	...시간 후에 ...si gan hu e
- a quarter of an hour	십 오분 후에 si bo bun hu e
- three quarters of an hour	사 십 오분 후에 sa si bo bun hu e
too early/late	너무 일찍/늦게 neo mu il jjik/neut ge
on time	정각에 jeong ga ge
summertime (daylight saving)	써머 타임 sseo meo ta im

1.4  One, two, three...

| 0 | 영
yeong |
| 1 | 일
il |

2	이	i
3	삼	sam
4	사	sa
5	오	o
6	육	yuk
7	칠	chil
8	팔	pal
9	구	gu
10	십	sip
11	십일	si bil
12	십이	si bi
13	십삼	sip sam
14	십사	sip sa
15	십오	si bo
16	십육	sim nyuk
17	십칠	sip chil
18	십팔	sip-pal
19	십구	sip-gu

20	이십	i sip
21	이십일	i si bil
22	이십이	i si bi
30	삼십	sam sip
31	삼십일	sam si bil
32	삼십이	sam si bi
40	사십	sa sip
50	오십	o sip
60	육십	yuk sip
70	칠십	chil sip
80	팔십	pal sip
90	구십	gu sip
100	백	baek
101	백일	bae gil
110	백십	baek sip
120	백이십	bae gi sip
200	이백	i baek
300	삼백	sam baek

400	사백	sa baek
500	오백	o baek
600	육백	yuk baek
700	칠백	chil baek
800	팔백	pal baek
900	구백	gu baek
1,000	천	cheon
1,100	천백	cheon baek
2,000	이천	i cheon
10,000	만	man
100,000	십 만	sim man
1,000,000	백 만	baeng-man
1st	첫 번째/ 첫째	cheot beon jjae/cheot jjae
2nd	두 번째/ 둘째	du beon jjae/dul jjae
3rd	세 번째/ 셋째	se beon jjae/set jjae
4th	네 번째/ 넷째	ne beon jjae/net jjae
5th	다섯 번째/ 다섯째	da seot beon jjae/da seot jjae

6th	여섯 번째/여섯째 yeo seot beon jjae/yeo seot jjae
7th	일곱 번째/일곱째 il gop beon jjae/il gop jjae
8th	여덟 번째/여덟째 yeo deol beon jjae/yeo deol jjae
9th	아홉 번째/아홉째 a hop beon jjae/a hop jjae
10th	열 번째/열째 yeol beon jjae/yeol jjae
11th	열 한번째 yeol han beon jjae
12th	열 두번째 yeol du beon jjae
13th	열 세번째 yeol se beon jjae
14th	열 네번째 yeol ne beon jjae
15th	열 다섯번째 yeol da seot beon jjae
16th	열 여섯번째 yeol yeo seot beon jjae
17th	열 일곱번째 yeol il gop beon jjae
18th	열 여덟번째 yeol yeo deol beon jjae
19th	열 아홉번째 yeol a hop beon jjae
20th	스무 번째 seu mu beon jjae
21st	스물 한 번째 seu mul han beon jjae
22nd	스물 두 번째 seu mul du beon jjae
30th	서른 번째 seo reun beon jjae

100th	백 번째 baek beon jjae
1,000th	천 번째 cheon beon jjae
once	한 번 han beon
twice	두 번 du beon
double	두 배 du bae
triple	세 배 se bae
half	반 ban
a quarter	사분의 일 sa bu nui il
a third	삼분의 일 sam bu nui il
some/a few	조금 jo geum
2 + 4 = 6	이 더하기 사는 육 i deo ha gi sa neun yuk
4 - 2 = 2	사 빼기 이는 이 sa bbae gi i neun i
2 x 4 = 8	이 곱하기 사는 팔 i go pa gi sa neun pal
4 ÷ 2 = 2	사 나누기 이는 이 sa na nu gi i neun i
even/odd	짝수/홀수 jjak su/hol su
total	합(계) hap(gye)
6 x 9	육 곱하기 구 yuk go pa gi gu

1.5 The weather

Is the weather going to be good/bad?	날씨가 좋을/나쁠까요? **Nal ssi ga joe-ul/na ppeul kka yo?**
Is it going to get colder/hotter?	날씨가 추울/더울까요? **Nal ssi ga chu ul/deo-ul kka yo?**
What temperature is it going to be?	기온이 얼마나 될까요? **Gi o ni eol ma na doel kka yo?**
Is it going to rain?	비가 올까요? **Bi ga ol kka yo?**
Is there going to be a storm?	폭풍이 올까요? **Pok pung-i ol kka yo?**
Is it going to snow?	눈이 올까요? **Nu ni ol kka yo?**
Is it going to freeze?	길이 얼을까요? **Gi li eo leul kka yo?**
Is the thaw setting in?	녹기 시작해요? **Nok gi si ja khe yo?**
Is it going to be foggy?	안개가 낄까요? **An gae ga kkil kka yo?**
Is there going to be a thunderstorm?	천둥이 칠까요? **Cheon dung i chil kka yo?**
The weather's changing	날씨가 바뀌고 있어요 **Nal ssi ga ba kkwi go it seo yo**
It's going to be cold	날이 추워질 거예요 **Na ri chu weo jil geo yeo yo**
What's the weather going to be like today/tomorrow?	오늘/내일 날씨는 어떨까요? **O neul/nae-il nal ssi neun eo tteol kka yo?**

무더운 sweltering/muggy	화창한 sunny	맑은 fine
서리 frost	밤 서리 overnight frost	얼음/길이 언 ice/icy
비 rain	강풍 gusts of wind	폭우/호우 downpour

쌀쌀한 frost/frosty	우박 hail	서늘한/시원한 cool
쾌청한 날 sunny day	숨막히게 더운 stifling	눈 snow
맑은/구름 낀/잔뜩 흐린 하늘 clear skies/cloudy/ overcast	적당한/강한/매우 강한 바람 moderate/strong/ very strong winds	구름이 낀/흐린 cloudiness 바람 wind
매우 더운 very hot	온화한 mild	바람 부는 windy
허리케인/태풍 hurricane	폭풍 storm	혹서 heatwave
맑은 fine/clear	춥고 습한 cold and damp	으스스한 bleak
폭우 heavy rain	안개/인개가 자욱한 fog/foggy	눅눅한/습한 humid
...도(영하/영상) ...degrees (below/ above zero)		

1.6 Here, there...

See also 5.1 Asking directions

here, over here / there, over there	여기/저기 yeo gi/jeo gi
somewhere/nowhere	어딘가에/아무데도 eo din-ga e/a mu de do
everywhere	어디에나 eo di e na
far away/nearby	멀리/가까이에(근처에) meol li/ga kka i e(geun cheo e)
(on the) right/(on the) left	오른 쪽/왼 쪽 o reun jjok/oen jjok
to the right/left of	오른 쪽으로/왼 쪽으로 o reun jjo g ro/oen jjo g ro

straight ahead	바로 앞 **ba ro ap**
via	...를 지나 **...reul ji na**
in	...안에 **...a ne**
to	...로 **...ro**
on	...위에 **...wi e**
under	...아래 **...a rae**
opposite/facing	맞은 편에 **ma jeun pyeo ne**
next to	...옆에 **...yeo pe**
near	...근처에 **...geun cheo-e**
in front of	...앞에 **...a pe**
in the center	가운데에 **ga un de e**
forward	앞으로 **a p ro**
down	아래로 **a rae ro**
up	위로 **wi ro**
inside	안의/안에 **a nui/a ne**
outside	바깥쪽의(에) **ba kkat jjo gui/ba kkat jjo ge**
behind	뒤에 **dwi e**
at the front	앞에 **a pe**

at the back	뒤에	dwi e
in the north	북 쪽에	buk jjo ge
to the south	남 쪽으로	nam jjo geu ro
from the west	서 쪽에서	seo jjo ge seo
from the east	동 쪽에서	dong jjo ge seo
to the...of	의...쪽으로	ui...jjo geu ro

1.7 What does that sign say?

See 5.2 Traffic signs

대여	for hire	식수	drinking water	호텔	hotel
매진	sold out	사용 금지	not in use	고장	out of order
대기실	waiting room	미시오	push	정지	stop
온수/냉수	hot/cold water	세 놓음	for rent	매물	for sale
비상 제동장치	emergency brake	화장실	bathrooms	우체국	post office
화재시 탈출구/에스칼레이터	fire escape/escalator	금연/쓰레기 투기 금지	no smoking/no litter	관광 안내소	tourist information bureau
고압	high voltage	시용 중	engaged	(시립) 경찰	(municipal) police
안내	information	당기시오	pull	현금 출납원	cashier
비상구	emergency exit	매표소	ticket office	위험/화재 위험	danger/fire hazard

영업 중 open	운행표 timetable	입구 entrance
입장 (무료) admission (free)	접근 금지/출입금지 no access/no entry	문 닫음 closed
소방서 fire department	경찰 police	만원 full
개 조심 beware of the dog	병원 hospital	예약석 reserved
페인트 주의 wet paint	환전 exchange	응급 처치 first aid/accident and emergency (hospital)
위험 danger	보행자 pedestrians	
교통 순경 traffic police	사냥/낚시 금지 no hunting/fishing	손대지 마시오 please do not disturb/touch

1.8 **Legal holidays**

● **National holidays** in Korea are:

January 1: New Year's Day 설날 **Seol nal**

January: Korean New Year's Day (Lunar) 설날 **Seol nal**

March 1: Samil Independence Movement Day 삼일절 **Sa mil jeol**
This celebrates the independence movement in 1919 against Japanese colonial rule.

April 5: Arbor Day 식목일 **Sing mo gil**
This is a day designated for planting trees at nearby mountains and parks.

April: Buddha's Birthday (Lunar) 석가탄신일 **Seok ka tan si nil**
This day celebrates the birth of Buddha; on the eve, a street parade with multi-colored lanterns is held.

May 5: Children's Day 어린이날 **Eo ri ni nal**

June 6: Memorial Day 현충일 **Hyeon chung-il**
This day pays tribute to those who sacrificed their lives for the country.

July 17: Constitution Day 제헌절 **Je heon jeol**

August 15: Liberation Day 광복절 **Gwang bok jeol**
This day celebrates Korea's liberation from Japanese colonization, which lasted 36 years.

August: Thanksgiving Day (Lunar) 추석 **Chu seok**
Chuseok is the most important traditional holiday; everyone heads for their hometown, so heavy traffic congestion on major highways should be expected for all three days.

October 3: National Foundation Day 개천절 **Gae cheon jeol**

December 25: Christmas Day 성탄절 **Seong tan jeol**

2 Meet and Greet

2. Meet and Greet

● **Koreans** greet each other with a little bow. Younger people are expected to make a deep bow to show their respect to the elderly. Handshakes are exchanged among adults, but it is not very acceptable when greeting a woman.

2.1 Greetings

Good morning/
  afternoon/evening

안녕하세요
An nyeong ha se yo

Hello Peter, how
  are things?

안녕하세요 피터씨 일은 잘 되세요?
An nyeong ha se yo pi teo ssi i reun jal doe se yo?

Hi Helen; fine,
  thank you, and you?

네 헬렌씨 안녕하세요?
Ne he len ssi an nyeong ha se yo?

Very well, and you?

네 어떻게 지내세요?
Ne eo ddeo kke ji nae se yo?

In excellent health/
  In great shape

네 잘지내요
Ne jal ji nae yo

So-so

그저 그래요
Geu jeo geu rae yo

Not very well

아주 좋지는 않네요
A ju jo chi neun an ne yo

Not bad

그냥 지내요
Geu nyang ji nae yo

I'm going to leave

가봐야 겠어요
Ga bwa ya ge sseo yo

I have to be going,
  someone's waiting
  for me

지금 누가 기다리고 있어서
가야겠어요
**Ji geum nu ga gi da ri go i sseo seo
ga ya ge sseo yo**

Good-bye

안녕히 가세요
An nyeong hi ga se yo

See you later

또 봐요
Tto bwa yo

See you soon	다시 봐요 Da si bwa yo
See you in a little while	조만간 다시 봐요 Jo man gan da si bwa yo
Sweet dreams	잘 자요 Jal ja yo
Good night	안녕히 주무세요 An nyeong hi ju mu se yo
All the best/Have fun	잘 지내세요 Jal ji nae se yo
Good luck	행운을 빌어요 Haeng-u neul bi reo yo
Have a nice vacation	휴가 잘 보내세요 Hu ga jal bo nae se yo
Bon voyage/Have a good trip	여행 잘 다녀 오세요 Yeo haeng jal da nyeo o se yo
Thank you, the same to you	고마워요, 잘 지내세요 Go ma wo yo, jal ji nae se yo
Say hello to/Give my regards to...	...에게 안부 전해 주세요 ...e ge an bu jeon hae ju se yo

2.2 Asking a question

Who?	누구? Nu gu?
Who's that?/Who is it?/ Who's there?	누구세요? Nu gu se yo?
What?	뭐예요? Mwo yeo yo?
What is there to see?	볼 것이 있나요? Bol ge si in na yo?
What category of hotel is it?	무슨 급 호텔이에요? Mu seun geup ho te ri e yo?
Where?	어디에요? Eo di e yo?

Where's the bathroom?	화장실이 어디에요? Hwa jang si ri eo di e yo?
Where are you going?	어디 가세요? Eo di ga se yo?
Where are you from?	어디서 왔어요? Eo di seo wa sseo yo?
How far is that?	얼마나 멀어요? Eol ma na meo reo yo?
How long does that take?	얼마나 걸려요? Eol ma na geol lyeo yo?
How long is the trip?	여행은 얼마나 걸리나요? Yeo haeng eun eo lma na geol li na yo?
How much?	얼마예요? Eol ma ye yo?
How much is this?	이거 얼마예요? I geo col ma ye yo?
What time is it?	몇 시예요? Myeot si ye yo?
Which one/s?	어느 것? Eo neu geot?
Which glass is mine?	어느 컵이 내거예요? Eo neu keo bi nae kkeo ye yo?
When?	언제요? Eon je yo?
When are you leaving?	언제 떠나요? Eon je ddeo na yo?
Why?	왜요? Wae yo?
Why are you leaving?	왜 가세요? Wae ga se yo?
Could you...?	알려주세요 ...a yeo ju se yo?
Could you help me/ give me a hand please?	(좀) 도와주세요 (Jom) do wa ju se yo
Could you come with me, please?	같이 좀 가 주세요 Ga chi jom ga ju se yo

Could you point that out to me/show me please?	어떻게 가는지 가르쳐 주세요 **Eo tteo ke ga neun ji ga reu chyeo ju se yo**
Could you reserve/book me some tickets please?	예약 좀 해 주세요 **Ye yak jom hae ju se yo**
Could you recommend another hotel?	다른 호텔을 좀 알려주세요 **Da reun ho te reul jom al lyeo ju se yo**
Do you know...?	...아세요? **...a se yo?**
Do you know whether...?	...인지 아세요? **...in ji a se yo?**
Do you have...?	...있어요? **...i sseo yo?**
Do you have a ... for me?	...있으세요? **I sseu se yo?**
Do you have a vegetarian dish, please?	채식 되나요? **Chae sik doe an yo?**
I would like...	...주세요 **...ju se yo**
I'd like a kilo of apples, please	사과 일 킬로 주세요 **Sa gwa il kil lo ju se yo**
Can/May I?	...돼요? **...dwae yo?**
Can/May I take this away?	이거 가져가도 돼요? **I geo ga jyeo ga do dwae yo?**
Can I smoke here?	여기서 담배 피워도 돼요? **Yeo gi seo dam bae pi wo do dwae yo?**
Could I ask you something?	뭐 좀 물어봐도 돼요? **Mwo jom mu reo bwa do dwae yo?**

 **2.3** How to reply

Yes, of course	네, 물론이죠 **Ne, mul lo ni jyo**
No, I'm sorry	죄송하지만 안 돼요 **Joe song-ha ji man an dwae yo**

Yes, what can I do for you?	네 뭘 도와드릴까요? **Ne, mwol do wa d ril kka yo?**
Just a moment, please	잠시만요 **Jam si ma nyo**
No, I don't have time now	아니오, 지금 시간이 없어요 **A ni yo, ji geum si ga ni eob seo yo**
No, that's impossible	아니오, 안돼요 **A ni yo, an dwae yo**
I think so/I think that's absolutely right	네, 맞아요 **Ne, ma ja yo**
I think so too/I agree	저도 그렇게 생각해요 **Jeo do geu reo ke saeng ga kae yo**
I agree/don't agree	네 그래요/그렇지 않아요 **Ne geu rae yo/geu reo chi a na yo**
OK/it's fine	네, 좋아요 **Ne, jo a yo**
OK, all right	네, 됐어요 **Ne, dwaet seo yo**
I hope so too	그랬으면 좋겠어요 **Geu rae sseu myeon jo ke sseo yo**
No, not at all/ Absolutely not	전혀 아니에요/절대로 아니에요 **Jeon hyeo a ni e yo/jeol dae ro a ni e yo**
No, no one	아니오, 아무도요 **A ni yo, a mu do yo**
No, nothing	아니오, 아무것도 아니에요 **A ni yo, a mu geot do a ni e yo**
That's right	맞아요 **Ma ja yo**
Something's wrong	뭐가 잘 못 됐어요 **Mwo ga jal mot dwae sseo yo**
Perhaps/maybe	아마도요 **A ma do yo**
I don't know	잘 모르겠어요 **Jal mo reu ge sseo yo**

2.4 Thank you

Thank you	고마워요 Go ma wo yo
Thank you for...	...해줘서 고마워요 ...hae jwo seo go ma wo yo
Thank you very much	감사합니다 Gam sa ham mi da
You shouldn't have	이렇게까지 해주셔서 감사합니다 I reo ke kka ji hae ju syeo seo gam sa ham mi da
I enjoyed it very much	즐거웠어요 Jeul geo wo sseo yo
You're welcome	괜찮아요/아니에요 Gwaen cha na yo/a ni e yo
My pleasure/ don't mention it	별 말씀을요 Beol mal sseu meul yo
That's all right	괜찮아요 Gwaen cha na yo
Excuse me (starting to speak to a stranger)	실례합니다 Sil lye ham mi da

2.5 I'm sorry

Excuse me/pardon
  (asking to repeat
  what's been said)
	뭐라고 하셨어요?
	Mwo ra go ha syeo sseo yo?

I'm sorry	죄송해요 Joe song hae yo
I do apologize	사과 드려요 Sa gwa deu ryeo yo
Sorry, I didn't know that...	죄송해요, ...몰랐어요 Joe song hae yo, ...mol la sseo yo
I didn't mean it/It was an accident	일부러 그런 건 아니에요 Il bu reo geu reon geon a ni e yo

That's all right/Don't worry about it	괜찮아요/걱정 마세요 Gwaen cha na yo/geok jeong ma se yo
Never mind/Forget it	아무 일도 아니에요 A mu il do a ni e yo
It could happen to anyone	그럴 수도 있죠 Geu reol su do it jyo

2.6 What do you think?

Which do you prefer/like best?	어떤 게 더 좋이요? Eo tteon ge deo jo a yo?
What do you think?	어떻게 생각해요? Eo tteo ke saeng ga khae yo?
Don't you like dancing?	춤 추는 거 좋아하지 않으세요? Chum chu neun geo jo a ha ji a neu se yo?
I don't mind	상관없어요 Sang-gwan eob seo yo
Great/Wonderful	훌륭해요/좋아요 Hul lyung hae yo/jo a yo
I'm very happy/delighted to...	...해서 좋아요 ...hae seo jo a yo
I'm glad that...	...해서 좋이요 ...hae seo jo a yo
It's really nice here	여기 참 좋네요 Yeo gi cham jon ne yo
How nice for you!	참 잘 됐군요 Cham jal dwaess gu nyo
I'm (not) very happy with...	...가 좋아요/싫어요 ...ga jo a yo/si reo yo
I'm having a great time	재미있어요 Jae mi i sseo yo
I can't wait till tomorrow/I'm looking forward to tomorrow	빨리 내일이 왔으면 좋겠어요 Ppal li nae i ri wa sseu myeon jo ke sseo yo

I hope it works out	잘 됐으면 좋겠어요 Jal dwae sseu myeon jo ke sseo yo
How awful!/What a pity!/ What a shame!	저런 Jeo reon
What nonsense/How silly/ That's ridiculous!	말도 안돼요 Mal do an dwae yo
How disgusting!	정말 끔찍해요 Jeong mal kkeum ji kae yo
I don't like it/them	마음에 안 들어요 Ma eu me an deu re yo
I'm fed up/bored	지겨워요 Ji gyeo wo yo
This is no good	이건 안 돼요 I geon an dwae yo
This is not what I expected	이건 아니지요 I geon a ni ji yo

3 Small Talk

3. Small Talk

 Introductions

May I introduce myself?	제 소개를 할게요 Je so ge reul hal kke yo
My name's...	제 이름은...입니다 Je i reu meun...im mi da
I'm...	저는...입니다 Jeo neun...im mi da
What's your name?	이름이 뭐에요? I reu mi mwo e yo?
May I introduce...?	...를 소개할게요 ...reul so ge hal kke yo
This is my wife/husband	제 처/남편이에요 Je cheo/nam pyeon-i e yo
This is my daughter/son	제 딸/아들입니다 Je ttar/a deur-im mi da
This is my mother/father	제 어머니/아버지이십니다 Je eo meo ni/a beo ji-sim mi da
This is my fiancée/fiancé	제 약혼녀/약혼자에요 Je ya kon nyeo/ya kon ja-e yo
This is my friend	제 친구에요 Je chin-gu e yo
How do you do?	만나서 반가워요 Ma na seo ban-ga wo yo
Hi, pleased to meet you	안녕하세요, 만나서 반가워요. An nyeong ha se yo, ma na seo ban-ga wo yo
Pleased to meet you	만나서 반갑습니다 Ma na seo ban-gap seum mi da
Where are you from?	어디서 왔어요? Eo di seo wa sseo yo?
I'm American	미국에서요 Mi gu ge seo yo

What city do you live in?	어느 도시에 살아요? Eo neu do si e sa ra yo?
in...near...	...근처...에 살아요 ...geun cheo ...e sa ra yo
Have you been here long?	여기 오래 있었어요? Yeo gi o rae i sseo sseo yo?
A few days	며칠 있었어요 Myeo chil i sseo sseo yo
How long are you staying here?	여기 얼마나 오래 계실 거에요? Yeo gi eol ma na o rae gye sil geo e yo?
We're (probably) leaving tomorrow/in two weeks	(아마) 내일/이 주 후에 떠날 거에요 (A ma) nae il/i ju hu e tteo nal geo e yo
Where are you staying?	어디에 계세요? Eo die gye se yo?
I'm staying in a hotel/ an apartment	호텔에/아파트에 있어요 Ho te re/a pa teu e i sseo yo
At a campsite	야잉장에 Ya yeong jang e
I'm staying with friends/ relatives	친구들/친척들하고 같이 있어요 Chin-gu deul/chin cheok deul ha go ga chi i sseo yo.
Are you here on your own?	여기에 혼자 있어요? Yeo gi e hon ja i sseo yo?
Are you here with your family?	가족과 함께 있어요? Ga jok gwa ham kke i sseo yo?
I'm on my own	혼자 있어요 Hon ja i sseo yo
I'm with my wife/ husband	처/남편과 같이 있어요 Cheo/nam pyeon-gwa ga chi i sseo yo
- with my family	-가족과 같이 있어요 ga jok kwa ga chi i sseo yo
- with relatives	-친척하고 있어요 chin cheo kha go i sseo yo
- with a friend/friends	-친구(들)와 같이 있어요 chin-gu(deul)wa ga chi i sseo yo
Are you married?	결혼 했어요? Gyeol hon hae sseo yo?

Are you engaged?	약혼 했어요? Ya khon hae sseo yo?
That's none of your business	상관 마세요 Sang-gwan ma se yo
I'm married	결혼 했어요 Gyeol hon hae sseo yo
I'm single	미혼 이에요 Mi ho ni e yo
I'm not married	결혼 안 했어요 Gyeol hon an hae sseo yo
I'm separated	별거 중이에요 Byeol geo jung i e yo
I'm divorced	이혼했어요 I hon hae sseo yo
I'm a widow/widower	혼자됐어요 Hon ja dwae sseo yo
Do you have any children/ grandchildren?	자녀는 어떻게 되세요/손자 는 있나요? Ja nyeo neun eo tteo ke doe se yo/ son ja neun in na yo?
How old are you?	몇 살이에요? Myeot sa ri e yo?
How old is she/he?	그 사람은 몇 살이에요? Geu sa ra meun myeot sa ri e yo?
I'm...(years old)	...살 이에요 ...sa ri e yo
She's/he's...(years old)	그 사람은...살 이에요 Geu sa ra meun...sa ri e yo
What do you do for a living?	무슨 일 하세요? Mu seu nil ha se yo?
I work in an office	사무실에서 일해요 Sa mu si re seo il hae yo
I'm a student	학생이에요 Hak saeng i e yo
I'm unemployed	일 안 해요 Il an hae yo

| I'm retired | 은퇴했어요 |
| | Eun toe hae sseo yo |

| I'm on a disability pension | 장애인 연금 받아요 |
| | Jang-ae in yeon geum ba da yo |

| I'm a housewife | 가정 주부에요 |
| | Ga jeong ju bu e yo |

| Do you like your job? | 직장일이 마음에 들어요? |
| | Jik jang-i li ma eu me deu reo yo? |

| Most of the time | 대부분은요 |
| | Dae bu bu neu nyo |

| Mostly I do, but I prefer vacations | 일도 좋아하지만, 휴가가 더 좋아요. |
| | Il do jo a ha ji man, hu ga ga deo jo a yo |

 3.2 I beg your pardon?

| I don't speak any/ I speak a little... | ...말은 전혀/조금밖에 못 해요 |
| | ...ma reun jeon hyeo/jo geum ba kke mo te yo |

| I'm American | 저는 미국 사람이에요 |
| | Jeo neun mi guk sa ra mi e yo |

| Do you speak English? | 영어 할 줄 아세요? |
| | Yeong-eo hal jjul a se yo? |

| Is there anyone who speaks...? | ...말 할 줄 아는 사람 있어요? |
| | ...mal hal jjul a neun sa ram i sseo yo? |

| I beg your pardon/ What? | 뭐라고 했어요? |
| | Mwo ra go hae sseo yo? |

| I don't understand | 잘 모르겠어요 |
| | Jal mo reu ge sseo yo |

| Do you understand me? | 알겠어요? |
| | Al ge sseo yo? |

| Could you repeat that, please? | 다시 말씀해 주세요 |
| | Da si mal sseum hae ju se yo |

| Could you speak more slowly, please? | 천천히 말씀해 주세요 |
| | Cheon cheon hi mal sseum hae ju se yo |

| What does that mean? | 그게 무슨 뜻이에요? |
| | Geu ge mu seun tteu si e yo? |

What does that word mean?	그 단어가 무슨 뜻이에요? **Geu da neo ga mu seun tteu si e yo?**
It's more or less the same as...	...와 비슷해요 **...wa bi seut hae yo**
Could you write that down for me, please?	그걸 적어 주시겠어요 **Geu geol jeo geo ju si ge sseo yo**
Could you spell that for me, please?	철자로 말해 주세요 **Cheol ja rol mal hae ju se yo**
Could you point that out in this phrase book, please?	이 책 어디에 적혀 있는지 가르쳐 주세요 **I chaek eo di e jeo kyeo in neun ji ga reu chyeo ju se yo**
Just a minute, I'll look it up	잠깐만요, 찾아 볼게요 **Jam kkan ma nyo, cha ja bol kke yo**
I can't find the word/ the sentence	그 단어를/문장을 찾을 수 없어요 **Geu da neo reul/mun jang-eul cha jeul su eop seo yo**
How do you say that in...?	...말로 그건 어떻게 말하나요? **...mal lo geu geon eo ddeo kke mal ha na yo?**
How do you pronounce that?	어떻게 발음하나요? **Eo tteo ke ba reum ha na yo?**

3.3 Starting/ending a conversation

Could I ask you something?	뭐 좀 물어봐도 돼요? **Mwo jom mu reo bwa do dwae yo?**
Excuse me	실례합니다 **Sil lye ham mi da**
Could you help me please?	좀 도와주시겠어요? **Jom do wa ju si ge sseo yo?**
Yes, what's the problem?	네, 무슨 일이세요? **Ne, mu seu ni ri se yo?**
Sorry, I don't have time now	죄송해요, 지금 시간이 없어요. **Joe song hae yo, ji geum si ga ni eop seo yo**

What can I do for you?	뭘 도와줄까요? Mwol do wa jul ga yo?
Do you have a light?	불 좀 빌릴 수 있을까요? Bul jom bil lil su i sseul kka yo?
May I join you?	같이 해도 돼요? Ga chi hae do dwae yo?
Could you take a picture of me/us?	사진 좀 찍어 줄래요? Sa jin jom jji geo jul lae yo?
Leave me alone	혼자 있게 해주세요 Hon ja iss ge hae ju se yo
Go away or I'll scream	저리 가세요 안 그러면 소리지를 거에요 Jeo ri ga se yo an geu reo myeon so ri ji reul geo e yo

3.4 A chat about the weather

See also 1.5 The weather

It's so hot/cold today!	오늘 참 더워요/추워요 O neul cham deo wo yo/chu wo yo
Isn't it a lovely day?	날씨 참 좋지 않아요? Nal ssi cham jo chi a na yo?
It's so windy/what a storm!	바람이 정말 많이 부네요 Ba ra mi jeong mal ma ni bu ne yo
All that rain/snow!	대단한 비/눈야 Daw dan han bi/nu ni ya
It's so foggy!	안개가 자욱해요 An gae ga ja u kae yo
Has the weather been like this for long?	날씨가 오랫동안 이랬나요? Nal ssi ga o raet dong.an i raen na yo?
Is it always this hot/cold here?	여긴 항상 이렇게 더운가요/추운가요? Yeo gin hang sang i reo ke deo un.ga yo/chu un.ga yo?
Is it always this dry/humid here?	여긴 항상 이렇게 건조한가요/습한가요? Yeo gin hang sang i reo ke geon jo han.ga yo/seu phan.ga yo?

45

3.5 Hobbies

Do you have any hobbies?	무슨 취미가 있으세요? **Mu seun chwi mi ga i sseu se yo?**
I like knitting/reading/ photography	뜨개질/책 읽기/사진찍기를 좋아해요 **Tteu gae jil/chae gil kki/sa jin jjik gi-reul jo a hae yo**
I enjoy listening to music	음악 듣는 걸 좋아해요 **Eu mak deun neun geol jo a hae yo**
I play the guitar/ the piano	기타를/피아노를 쳐요 **Gi ta reul/pi a no reul cheo yo**
I like the cinema	영화를 좋아해요 **Yeong hwa reul jo a hae yo**
I like traveling/playing sports/going fishing/ going for a walk	여행/운동/낚시/산책을 좋아해요. **Yeo haeng/un dong/nak ssi/ san chag-eul jo a hae yo**
Korean drama/pop music is popular in other countries.	한국 드라마가/대중음악이 외국에서 인기가 있어요. **Han guk d ra ma-ga/dae jung eu ma g-i oe guk-e so in gi ga i seo yo.**
I am a fan of the figure skater "Yuna Kim."	피겨 선수 "김연아"의 팬이에요. **Fi gure seon su "Kim Yu na"-ui fan-i e yo.**
My hobby is playing computer games.	컴퓨터 게임이 제 취미예요. **Com pu ter ga me-i je chwi mi ye yo.**
I listen to Korean Pop a lot on my mp3 player.	한국 음악을 mp3 플레이어로 많이 들어요. **Han guk eu ma geul mp3 player-ro ma ni deu reo yo.**

3.6 Invitations

Would you like to go dancing with me?	저와 함께 춤추러 가실래요? **Jeo wa ham kke chum chu reo ga sil lae yo?**
Would you like to have lunch/dinner with me?	저와 함께 점심/저녁 드실래요? **Jeo wa ham kke jeom sim/jeo nyeok deu sil lae yo?**

Would you like to go out with me?	저와 함께 외출 할래요? Jeo wa ham kke oe chul hal lae yo?
Would you like to come to the beach with me?	저와 같이 해변에 가실래요? Jeo wa ga chi hae byeo ne ga sil lae yo?
Would you like to come into town with us?	우리하고 시내에 가실래요? U ri ha go si nae e ga sil lae yo?
Would you like to come and see some friends with us?	같이 친구 만나러 갈래요? Ga chi chin-gu man na reo gal lae yo?
Shall we dance?	춤 추실까요? Chum chu sil kka yo?
- sit at the bar?	–바에 앉을까요? ba.e an jeul kka yo?
- get something to drink?	–마실까요? ma sil kka yo?
- go for a walk/drive?	–산책하러/드라이브 갈까요? san chae ka reo/d ra i beu gal kka yo?
Yes, all right	네, 좋아요 Ne, jo a yo
Good idea	좋은 생각이에요 Jo eun saeng-ga gi e yo
No thank you	고맙지만 사양할께요 Go map ji man sa yang hal kke yo
Maybe later	나중에요 Na jung-e yo
I don't feel like it	별로 내키지 않아요 Byeol lo nae ki ji a na yo
I don't have time	시간이 없어요 Si ga ni eop seo yo
I already have a date	데이트가 있어요 De i teu ga i sseo yo
You look great	근사한데요 Geun sa han de yo
I'm not very good at dancing/volleyball/ swimming	춤을 잘 못 춰요/배구를 잘 못 해요/수영을 잘 못해요 Chu meul jal mot chwo yo/bae gu reul jal mot hae yo/su yeong eul jal mot hae yo

3.7 Paying a compliment

I like your car
차가 참 좋네요
Cha ga cham jon ne yo

I like your ski outfit
스키 장비가 참 좋네요
Seu ki jang bi ga cham jon ne yo

You are very nice
당신 참 좋은 사람이에요
Dang sin cham jo eun sa ra mi e yo

What a good boy/girl!
정말 착하군요
Jeong mal cha ka gu nyo

You're a good dancer
춤을 잘 추네요
Chu meul jal chwo ne yo

You're a very good cook
요리를 아주 잘 하네요
Yo ri reul a ju jal ha ne yo

You're a good soccer player
축구를 아주 잘 하네요
Chuk gu reul a ju jal ha ne yo

I like being with you
당신하고 같이 있는 게 좋아요
Dang sin ha go ga chi in neun.ge jo a yo

3.8 Intimate comments/questions

I've missed you so much
정말 보고 싶었어요
Jeong mal bo go si peo sseo yo

I dreamt about you
당신 꿈을 꿨어요
Dang sin kku meul kkwo sseo yo

I think about you all day
하루 종일 당신 생각을 해요
Ha ru jong-il dang sin saeng-ga geul hae yo

I've been thinking about you all day
하루 종일 당신 생각을 했어요
Ha ru jong-il dang sin saeng-ga geul hae sseo yo

You have such a sweet smile
당신은 미소가 정말 아름다워요
Dang si neun mi so ga jeong mal a reum da wo yo

You have such beautiful eyes
당신은 눈이 정말 아름다워요
Dang si neun ye bbeun nu ni jeong mal a reum da wo yo

I'm in love with you	당신을 사랑해요 Dang si neul sa rang hae yo
I'm in love with you too	나도 당신을 사랑해요 Na do dang si neul sa rang hae yo
I love you	당신이 좋아요 Dang si ni jo a yo
I love you too	저도요 Jeo do yo
I don't feel as strongly about you	당신에 대해 별다른 느낌이 없어요 Dang si ne dae hae byeol da reun neu kki mi eop seo yo
I already have a girlfriend/boyfriend	전 이미 여자친구/남자친구가 있어요. Jeon i mi yeo ja chin-gu/nam ja chin- gu ga i sseo yo
I'm not ready for that	아직은 안 돼요. A ji keun an dwae yo
I don't want to rush into it	서두르고 싶지 않아요 Seo du reu go sip ji a na yo
Take your hands off me	손 대지 말아요 Son dae ji ma ra yo
Okay, no problem	그럴께요 Geu leol kke yo
Will you spend the night with me?	같이 밤을 지낼래요? Ga chi ba meul ji nael lae yo?
I'd like to go to bed with you	당신과 자고 싶어요 Dang sin.gwa Ja go si peo yo
Only if we use a condom	콘돔을 사용한다면요 Kon do meul sa yong.han da.myeo nyo
We have to be careful about AIDS	에이즈를 조심해야 해요 E i jeu reul jo sim hae ya hae yo
That's what they all say	그건 사람들이 늘상 하는 말이구요 Geu geon sa ram deu li neul sang ha neun ma ri gu yo
We shouldn't take any risks	위험한 건 안돼요 Wi heom han geon an dwae yo
Do you have a condom?	콘돔 있어요? Kon dom i sseo yo?

Say hello to...	...인사 전해 주세요 **In sa jeon hae ju se yo**
All the best	잘 지내세요 **Jal ji nae se yo**
Good luck	행운을 빌어요 **Haeng-u neul bi reo yo**
When will you be back?	언제 돌아오세요? **Eon je do ra o se yo?**
I'll be waiting for you	기다리고 있을게요 **Gi da ri go i sseul kke yo**
I'd like to see you again	또 봤으면 좋겠어요 **Tto bwa sseu myeon jo ke sseo yo**
I hope we meet again soon	곧 다시 볼 수 있으면 좋겠어요 **Got da si bol su i sseu myeon jo ke sseo yo**
Here's our address, if you're ever in the United States...	우리 주소예요, 미국에 오면... **U ri ju so ye yo, mi gu ge o myeon...**
You'd be more than welcome	언제나 환영이에요 **Eon je na hwa nyeong-i e yo**

4 Eating out

4. Eating out

 At the restaurant

I'd like to reserve a table for seven o'clock, please	일곱 시에 예약을 하고 싶은데요 **Il gop si e ye ya geul ha go si peun de yo**
A table for two, please	두 사람 테이블 부탁합니다 **Du sa ram te i beul bu ta kam mi da**
We've reserved	예약했어요 **Ye yak hae sseo yo**
We haven't reserved	예약 안 했어요 **Ye yak an hae sseo yo**
Is the restaurant open yet?	식당이 이미 열었나요? **Sik dang i i mi yeo reon na yo?**
What time does the restaurant open?	몇 시에 여나요? **Myeot si e yeo na yo?**
What time does the restaurant close?	몇 시에 닫나요? **Myeot si e dan na yo?**
Can we wait for a table?	자리를 기다려도 될까요? **Ja ri reul gi da ryeo ro doel kka yo?**
Do we have to wait long?	오래 기다려야 하나요? **O rae gi da reo ya ha na yo?**
Is this seat taken?	이 자리에 누가 있나요? **I ja ri e nu ga in na yo?**
Could we sit here/there?	여기/저기 앉아도 될까요? **Yeo gi/jeo gi an ja do doel kka yo?**
Can we sit by the window?	창문 쪽에 앉아도 될까요? **Chang mun jjo ge an ja do doel kka yo?**
Are there any tables outside?	바깥에도 테이블이 있나요? **Ba kka te do te i beu ri in na yo?**
Do you have another chair for us?	여분의 의자가 있을까요? **Yeo bu nui ui ja ga i sseul kka yo?**
Do you have a highchair?	유아용 의자가 있나요? **Yu a yong ui ja ga in na yo?**

Is there a socket for this bottle-warmer?	우유병 데울 소켓이 있나요? U yu byeong de ul so ke si in na yo?
Could you warm up this bottle/jar for me?	이 병을 좀 데워주세요 I byeong.eul jom de wo ju se yo
Not too hot, please	너무 뜨겁지 않게 해 주세요 Neo mu tteu geop ji an ke hae ju se yo

예약 하셨나요?	Do you have a reservation?
성함이 어떻게 되시죠?	What name, please?
이쪽입니다	This way, please
이 자리는 예약이 된 자리에요	This table is reserved
십 오분 안에 한 자리가 빌 것입니다	We'll have a table free in fifteen minutes
기다리시겠습니까?	Would you like to wait (at the bar)?

| Is there somewhere I can change the baby's diaper? | 기저귀 갈아 줄 곳이 있나요?
Gi jeo gwi ga ra jul go si in na yo? |
| Where are the restrooms? | 화장실은 어디에 있어요?
Hwa jang si reun eo di e i sseo yo? |

4.2 Ordering

We'd like something to eat/drink	뭘 좀 머있으면/미셨으면 좋겠이요 Mwol jom meo geo sseu myeon/ ma syeo sseu myeon jo ke sseo yo
Could I have a quick meal?	빨리 되는 음식으로 주세요 Ppal li doe neun eum si geu ro ju se yo
We don't have much time	시간이 별로 없어요 Si ga ni byeol lo eop seo yo
We'd like to have a drink first	음료수 먼저 주세요 Eum nyo su meon jeo ju se yo
Could we see the menu/ wine list, please?	메뉴/포도주 목록을 좀 보여주시겠어요? Me nyu/po do ju mong no geul jom bo yeo ju se yo

Do you have a menu in English?	영어로 된 메뉴판이 있나요? **Yeong eo ro doen me nyu pa ni in na yo?**
Do you have a dish of the day/a tourist menu?	오늘의 특별 메뉴/여행자용 메뉴가 있나요? **O neul rui teuk byeol me nyu/yeo haeng ja yong me nyu ga in na yo?**
We haven't made a choice yet	아직 정하지 못했어요 **A jik jeong ha ji mot ha sseo yo**
What do you recommend?	어떤 걸 추천해 주시겠어요? **Eo tteon geol chu cheon hae u si ge sseo yo?**
What are the local specialities/your specialities?	이 지방의/이 식당의 특선요리는 뭐에요? **I ji bang.ui/i sik dang.ui teuk seon yo ri neun mwo e yo?**
I like strawberries/olives	딸기/올리브 주세요 **Ttal gi/o li beu ju se yo**
I don't like meat/fish	고기는/생선은 별로 안 좋아해요 **Go gi neun/saeng seo neun byeol lo an jo a hae yo**
What's this?	이게 뭔가요? **I ge mwon.ga yo?**
Does it have...in it?	여기에...이 들어있나요? **Yeo gi e...i deu reo in na yo?**
Is it stuffed with...?	속에...이 들어있나요? **So ge...i deu reo in na yo?**
What does it taste like?	맛이 어때요? **Ma si eo ddae yo?**
Is this a hot or a cold dish?	이건 따뜻한 요리인가요 차가운 요리인가요? **I geon tta deu tan yo ri in-ga yo cha ga un yo ri in-ga yo?**
Is this sweet?	이건 단가요? **I geon dan-ga yo?**
Is this hot/spicy?	이거 매워요? **I geo mae wo yo?**

무엇을 드시겠습니까?   What would you like?
정하셨어요?   Have you decided?
음료를 먼저 드릴까요?   Would you like a drink first?
어떤 음료를 드릴까요?   What would you like to drink?
...가 모자라요/다 나갔어요   We've run out of...
맛 있게 드세요   Enjoy your meal/Bon appetit
더 필요한 것 있으세요?   Is everything all right?
식탁을 치워 드릴까요?   May I clear the table?

Do you have anything else, by any chance?	혹시 다른 깃이 있나요? **Hok si da reun geo si in na yo?**
I'm on a salt-free diet	무염식 중이에요 **Mu yeom sik jung.i e yo**
I can't eat pork	돼지 고기를 못 먹어요 **Dwae ji go gɪ reul mot meo geo yo**
I can't have sugar	설탕 못 먹어요 **Seol tang mot meo geo yo**
I'm on a fat-free diet	무지방 식이요법 중이에요 **Mu ji bang si gi yo ppeop jung i e yo**
I can't have spicy food	매운 음식을 못 먹어요 **Mae un-eum si geul mot meo geo yo**
We'll have what those people are having	저쪽 사람들이 먹는 걸로 주세요 **Jeo jjok sa ram deu ri meong neun geol lo ju se yo**
I'd like...	...주세요 **...ju se yo**
We're not having...	...은 안 먹을게요 **...eun an meo geul kke yo**
Could I have some more bread, please?	빵 좀 더 주세요 **Ppang jom deo ju se yo**
Could I have another bottle of water/wine, please?	물/포도주 한 병 더 주세요 **Mul/po do ju han byeong deo ju se yo**
Could I have another portion of..., please?	...하나 더 추가해 주세요 **...ha na deo chu ga hae ju se yo**

Could I have the salt and pepper, please?	소금하고 후추 주세요
	So geum ha go hu chu ju se yo
Could I have a napkin, please?	냅킨 좀 주시겠어요
	Naep kin jom ju si ge sseo yo
Could I have a teaspoon, please?	차 숟가락 좀 주세요
	Cha su kka rak jom ju se yo
Could I have an ashtray, please?	재떨이 좀 주세요
	Jae tteo ri jom ju se yo
Could I have some matches, please?	성냥 좀 주시겠어요
	Seong nyang jom ju si ge sseo yo
Could I have some toothpicks, please?	이쑤시개 좀 주시겠어요
	I ssu si gae jom ju si ge sseo yo
Could I have a glass of water, please?	물 한 잔 주시겠어요
	Mul han jan ju si ge sseo yo
Could I have a straw please?	빨대 좀 주세요
	Ppal ttae jom ju se yo
Enjoy your meal/ Bon appetit	식사 맛있게 하세요
	Sik ssa ma si kke ha se yo
You too!	맛 있게 드세요
	Ma si kke deu se yo
Cheers!	건배
	Geon bae
The next round's on me	다음에는 제가 낼게요
	Da eu me neun je ga nael kke yo
Could we have a doggy bag, please?	남은 거 좀 싸 주시겠어요
	Na meun geo jom ssa ju si ge sseo yo?

4.3 The bill

See also 8.2 Settling the bill

How much is this dish?	얼마에요?
	Eol ma e yo?
Could I have the bill, please?	계산서 좀 주세요
	Gye san seo jom ju se yo
All together	한꺼번에 계산할게요
	Han kkeo beo ne gye san hal kke yo

Everyone pays separately/ let's go Dutch	각자 따로 계산합시다 Gak ja tta ro gye san hap si da
Could we have the menu again, please?	메뉴판을 다시 갖다 주세요 Me nyu pa neul da si gat da ju se yo
The...is not on the bill	...가 계산에서 빠졌어요 ...ga gye sa ne seo ppa jyeo sseo yo

4.4 Complaints

It's taking a very long time	시간이 너무 오래 걸리네요 Si ga ni neo mu o rae geol li ne yo
We've been here an hour already	우리가 여기 한 시간이나 있었어요 U ri ga yeo gi han si ga ni na i sseo sseo yo
This must be a mistake	뭔가 잘 못 됐네요 Mwon.ga jal mot doe ne yo
This is not what I ordered	이건 제가 주문한 게 아닌데요 I geon je ga ju mun han ge a nin de yo
I ordered...	...를 주문했어요 ...reul ju mun hae sseo yo
There's a dish missing	요리 한 가지가 빠졌어요. Yo ri han ga ji ga ppa jeo sseo yo
This is broken/not clean	이건 부서졌어요/ 이건 깨끗하지 잃아요 I geon bu seo jeo sseo yo/i geon kkae kkeu ta ji a na yo
The food's cold	음식이 식었어요 Eum si gi si geo sseo yo
The food's not fresh	음식이 신선하지 않아요 Eum si gi sin seon ha ji a na yo
The food's too salty/ sweet/spicy	이 음식은 너무 짜요/너무 달아요/너무 매워요 I eum si geun neo mu jja yo/neo mu da ra yo/neo mu mae wo yo
The meat's too rare	고기가 너무 덜 익었어요 Go gi ga neo mu deo ri geo sseo yo

The meat's overdone	고기를 너무 익혔네요 Go gi reul neo mu i kyeon ne yo
The meat's tough	고기가 질겨요 Go gi ga jil gyeo yo
The meat is off/ has gone bad	고기가 상했어요 Go gi ga sang hae sseo yo
Could I have something else instead of this?	이거 대신 다른 걸로 주세요 I geo dae sin da reun geol lo ju se yo
The bill/this amount is not right	계산이 잘 못 됐어요 Gye sa ni jal mot dwae sseo yo
We didn't have this	이건 안 먹었는데요 I geon an meo geon neun de yo
There's no toilet paper in the restroom	화장실에 휴지가 없어요. Hwa jang si re hu ji ga eop seo yo
Will you call the manager, please?	지배인을 불러주세요. Ji bae i neul bul leo ju se yo

4.5 Paying a compliment

That was a wonderful meal	맛있게 잘 먹었습니다 Ma si kke jal meo geo sseum mi da
The food was excellent	음식이 너무 맛있었어요 Eum si gi neo mu ma si sseo sseo yo
The...in particular was delicious	특히...이 맛있네요 Teu ki...i ma sin ne yo

4.6 The menu

전채 starter/hors d'oeuvres	주류 liqueur (after dinner)	후식류/차 desserts/ tea	채식 vegetable dishes
탕류 soups	메인 코스 main course	스낵_ snacks	특선요리 specialties
면류 noodles	전골류 hot pots	음료 drinks	파스타 pasta

육류	생선류	샐러드	피자
meat	fish	salad	pizza

닭요리	빵		
poultry	bread		

4.7 Alphabetcal list of dishes

● **Koreans food** is invigorating and varied, with many regions having their own specialities. If you want to taste a variety of dishes in one meal, then try *hanjeongsik*. This set meal usually consists of two types of soup, ten side dishes, and five types of vegetables and fish.

Bibimbap is assorted vegetables on steamed rice with red pepper paste sauce.

Bulgogi is one of the most popular Korean foods. Thin slices of beef are marinated in soy sauce and sesame oil and cooked on a dome-shaped grill.

Galbi (ribs) is another very popular Korean food. The ingredients are as same as for *bulgogi*, but a barbeque grill is used for *galbi*.

Kimchi is an important part of any Korean meal and is made of a spicy mixture of fermented vegetables (most often napa cabbage), chilli, garlic, ginger and other seasonings.

Naengmyeon is the most highly preferred summer dish. It is noodles served with cold beef broth. *Hamheung-naengmyeon*, a variation of *naengmyeon*, is just noodles and hot pepper paste sauce, without broth. There are many places specializing in *naengmyeon* in major cities.

Samgyetang (ginseng chicken soup) is the dish for summer in Korea. Especially on Chobok, Jungbok, and Malbok (days that mark the first, middle and last periods of the summer doldrums), people eat *samgyetang* to beat the summer heat.

Seolleongtang is a beef broth soup with chopped scallions. It is served with rice and it goes very well with *kkakttugi*, radish *kimchi*.

Shinseolo is a delicious mixture of beef and vegetables cooked in a steamboat pot.

Songpyeon are small cakes made of rice-flour dough with a filling of sweetened chestnuts and green mung beans. They are a traditional part of Chuseok, the Korean thanksgiving holiday.

5 Getting Around

5. Getting Around

● **In Korea**, cars are driven on the right side of the road and main streets can be very crowded from early morning until late evening. Due to the heavy traffic and often confusing road systems, it may be desirable to hire a driver along with the car, especially in large cities. Travelers who wish to hire a chauffeur-driven car must be prepared to pay the driver's meals and other traveling expenses as well.

Bicycle paths are rare in Korea. Though bikes can be hired in most towns, bikes are not often considered a proper means of transportation on main roads.

5.1 Asking directions

Excuse me, could I ask you something?	실례합니나, 뭐 좀 여쒀 몰게요 **Sil lye ham mi da, mwo jjom yeo jjwo bol kke yo**
I've lost my way	길을 잃었어요 **Gi reul i reo sseo yo**
Is there a ...around here?	이 근처에...가 있나요? **I geun cheo e...ga in na yo?**
Is this the way to...?	이쪽이...로 가는 길이 맞나요? **I jjo gi...ro ga neun gl ri man na yo?**
Could you tell me how to get to...?	...로 어떻게 갈 수 있는지 알려주세요 **...ro eo tteo ke gal su in neun ji al lyeo ju se yo**
What's the quickest way to...?	...로 가는데 제일 빠른 길이 어딘가요? **...ro ga neun de je il ppa reun gi ri eo din-ga yo?**
How many kilometers is it to...?	...까지 몇 킬로미터인가요? **...kka ji myeot kil lo mi teo in ga yo?**
Could you point it out on the map?	지도에서 어디인지 가리켜 주세요 **Ji do e seo eo di in ji ga ri kyeo ju se yo**

여기서 어디로 가야 할 지 잘
　모르겠어요
길을 잘 못 드셨어요
다시... 쪽으로 돌아가야 해요
저기에서부터 표지판을 따라
　가세요
저기 가서 다시 물어보세요

I don't know my way around
　here
You're going the wrong way
You have to go back to...
From there on just follow the
　signs
When you get there, ask again

직진 go straight ahead	우회전 turn right	건넘 cross
길 / 로 the road/street	터널 the tunnel	건물 the building
강 the river	교량 the bridge	길모퉁이에서 at the corner
좌회전 Turn left	이쪽으로 Follow	화살표 the arrow
기차 건널목 the grade crossing	양보 the 'yield' sign	고가도로 the overpass
교차로 the intersection/ 　crossroads	신호등 the traffic light	

5.2 Traffic signs

터널 내 점등 turn on headlights	갓길 사용금지 impassible shoulder	커브 curves
접근 금지/통행 금지 no access/no 　pedestrian access	관리자 상근 주차장 supervised garage/ 　parking lot	교차로 intersection/ 　crossroads
정지 stop	유료 주차장 paying carpark	위험 danger(ous)
인도 / 보도 sidewalk	우측통행/좌측통행 keep right/left	우회 detour

도로 서비스
road assistance
  (breakdown service)

낙석 주의
beware, falling rocks

차량 정비소
service station

방해하지 마시오.
do not obstruct

파손 도로
broken/uneven
  surface

우천시...킬로
rain or ice for...kms

최대 높이
maximum headroom

도로 폐쇄
road closed

대형 트럭
heavy trucks

통행료
toll payment

좁아짐
road narrows

일시 주차
parking for a limited
  period

우회전/좌회전 금지
no right/left turn

차선 변경
change lanes

기차 건널목
grade crossing

스노우 체인 부착
snow chains
  required

도로 끝
road closed

도로 공사
road works

출구
exit

비상시 차선
emergency lane

진입로
driveway

최대 속도
maximum speed

...외 주차 금지
parking reserved
  for...

도로 통제
road blocked

우선권
right of way

주의/조심
beware

파킹 디스크
parking disk
  (compulsory)

진입 금지
no entry

서행
slow down

견인지역
tow-away area

통행 금지
no passing

일반 통행
one way

주차금지
no parking

5.3 The car

See the diagram on page 67

5.4 The gas station

How many kilometers to the next gas station, please?	다음 주유소까지는 몇 킬로인가요? **Da eum ju yu so kka ji neun myeot kil lo in-ga yo?**
I would like...liters of	...리터 넣어주세요 **...ri teo neo eo ju se yo**

The parts of a car

(the diagram shows the numbered parts)

1	battery	배터리	bae teo ri
2	rear light	미등	mi deung
3	rear-view mirror	백미러	baek mi reo
	backup light		bakeop rait
4	aerial	안테나	an te na
	car radio	카 라디오	ca radio
5	gas tank	연료 탱크	yeol lyo taen k
6	spark plugs	스파크 플러그	s pa keu peul leo geu
	fuel pump	연료 펌프	yeol lyo peom peu
7	side mirror	사이드 미러	sa i deu mi reo
8	bumper	범퍼	beom peo
	carburettor	카뷰레터/기화기	ca byu re teo/gi hwa gi
	crankcase	크랭크 케이스	keu rang k ke i seu
	cylinder	실린더	sil lin deo
	ignition	시동	si dong
	warning light	경보등	gyeong bo deung
	generator	제너레이터	je neo ra i teo
	accelerator	액셀러레이터/가속장치	aek sel leo ra teo/ga sok jang chi
	handbrake	핸드브레이크	haen d b re i keu
	valve	밸브	bael beu
9	muffler	소음기	so eum gi
10	trunk	트렁크	teu reong keu
11	headlight	해드라이트/전조등	hae d ra i teu/jeon jo deung
	crank shaft	크랭크 축	k raen k chuk
12	air filter	에어 필터	e eo pil teo
	fog lamp	안개등	an-gae deong
13	engine block	엔진 블록	en jin beul lok
	camshaft	캠축	kaem chuk
	oil filter/pump	오일필터/펌프	o il pil teo/peom peu
	dipstick	오일 스틱	o il seu tik
	pedal	페달	pe dal
14	door	도어	do eo
15	radiator	냉각기	naeng-gak ki
16	brake disc	브레이크 디스크	b re i keu di seu keu
	spare wheel	스페어 바퀴	s pe eo ba kkwi
17	indicator	계기판	gye gi pan
18	windshield	앞 유리	am nyu ri
	wiper	와이퍼	wa i peo
19	shock absorbers	쇼크 업저버/	so keu eop seeo beo/
		충격 흡수체	chung-gyeok heup su che
	sunroof	선루프	seon ru p
	spoiler	스포일러	seu po il leo
20	steering column	스티어링 컬럼	seu ti eo ring keol leom
	steering wheel	핸들	haen deul

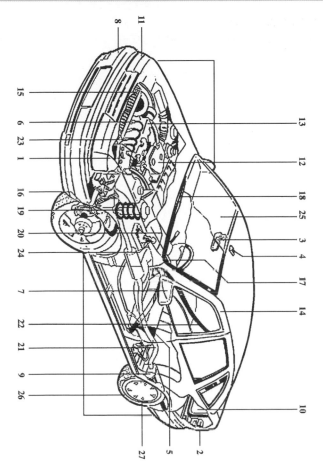

21	exhaust pipe	배기관	bae gi gwan
22	seat belt	안전 벨트	an jeon bel teu
	fan	팬/환풍기	pan/hwan pung-gi
23	distributor	배전기	bae jeon-gi
	cables	케이블	ke i beul
24	gear shift	기어	gi eo
	water pump		
25	windshield	앞 유리	am nyu ri
26	wheel	워터 펌프	wo teo peom peu
27	hubcap	바퀴	ba kwi
	piston	휠캡	wil kaep
		피스톤	pi seu ton

super	수퍼
	su peo
leaded	유연
	u yeon
unleaded	무연
	mu yeon
diesel	디젤
	di jel
...worth of gas	...리터 어치
	...ri teo eo chi
Fill her up, please	가득 채워 주세요
	Ga deuk chae wo ju se yo
Could you check the oil level, please?	오일을 점검해 주세요
	O i leul jeom geom hae ju se yo
Could you check the tire pressure, please?	타이어 압력을 점검해 주세요
	Ta i eo am nyeo geul jeom geom hae ju se yo
Could you change the oil, please?	오일을 바꿔주세요
	O i leul ba kkwo ju se yo
Could you clean the windshield, please?	앞 유리를 닦아 주세요
	Am nyu ri reul da kka ju se yo
Could you wash the car, please?	세차 해 주세요
	Se cha hae ju se yo

5.5 Breakdowns and repairs

I've broken down, could you give me a hand?	고장이 났는데, 좀 도와주세요
	Go jang-i nan neun de, jom do wa ju se yo.
I've run out of gas	기름이 다 떨어져가요
	Gi reu mi da tteo reo jeo ga yo
I've locked the keys in the car	열쇠를 두고 차 문을 잠갔어요
	Yeol soe leul du go cha meu neul jam ga sseo yo

The car/motorbike/ moped won't start	차/오토바이/모터 자전거가 출발이 안 돼요 Cha/o to bai/mo teu ja jeon-geo-ga chul ba ri an dwe yo
Could you contact the breakdown service for me, please?	수리 서비스 에 연락 좀 해 주세요 Su ri seo bi seu e yeol lak jom hae ju se yo
Could you call a garage for me, please?	카 센터에 전화 좀 해 주세요 Ka ssen teo e jeon hwa jom hae ju se yo
Could you give me a lift to the nearest garage?	가까운 정비소까지 좀 데려다 주세요 Ga kka un jeong bi so kka ji jom de ryeo da ju se yo
Could you give me a lift to the nearest town?	가까운 시내까지 좀 데려다 주세요 Ga kka un si nae kka ji jom de ryeo da ju se yo
Could you give me a lift to the nearest telephone booth?	가까운 전화박스까지 좀 데려다 주세요 Ga kka un jeon hwa bak seu kka ji jom de ryeo da ju se yo
Could you give me a the nearest emergency phone?	가까운 긴급 전화기 있는 곳에 좀 데려다 주세요 Ga kka un gin-geup jeon hwa gi in neun go se jom de ryeo da ju se yo
Can we take my moped?	제 모터 자전거를 가지고 가도 돼요? Je mo teu ja jeon-geo reul ga ji go ga do dwae yo?
Could you tow me to a garage?	정비소까지 견인해 주세요 Jeong bi soe kka ji gyeo nln hae ju se yo
There's probably something wrong with... (See pages 66-67)	...에 문제가 있는 것 같아요 ...e mun je ga in neun geot ga ta yo
Can you fix it?	고칠 수 있나요? Go chil su ln na yo?
Could you fix my tire?	타이어를 좀 고쳐 주세요 Ta i eo reul go chyeo ju se yo
Could you change this wheel?	이 바퀴를 바꿔 주세요 I ba kwi reul ba kkwo ju se yo

Can you fix it so it'll get me to...?	…까지 갈 수 있도록 고칠 수 있어요? …kka ji gal su i tto rok go chil su i sseo yo?
Which garage can help me?	어떤 정비소로 가면 되나요? Eo ddeon jeong bi so ro ga myeon doe na yo?
When will my car/ bicycle be ready?	차/자전거 수리가 언제까지 될까요? Cha/ja jeon-geo su ri ga eon je kka ji doel kka yo?
Have you finished yet?	벌써 끝내셨어요? Beol sseo kkeun nae syeo sseo yo?
Can I wait for it here?	여기서 기다려도 될까요? Yeo gi seo gi da ryeo do doe yo?
How much will it cost?	얼마 정도가 들까요? Eol ma jeong do ga deul kka yo?
Could you itemize the bill?	청구서에 항목별로 써 주세요 Cheong-gu seo e hang mok byeol lo sseo ju se yo
Could you give me a receipt for insurance purposes?	보험 처리 할 영수증을 주세요 Bo heom cheo ri hal yeong su jeung-eul ju se yo

5.6 Motorcycles and bicycles

See the diagram on page 73

● **Bicycle paths** are common in towns and cities and their use is strongly recommended. Bikes can usually be rented at tourist centers. The maximum speed for mopeds is 40 km/h both inside and outside town centers. Crash helmets are compulsory.

| 손님 차/자전거 부품이 없습니다 | I don't have parts for your car/ bicycle |
| 다른 곳에서 부품을 가져 와야 해요 | I have to get the parts from somewhere else |

부품을 주문해야 해요	I have to order the parts
반나절 걸릴 거에요	That'll take half a day
하루 정도 걸릴 거에요	That'll take a day
며칠 걸릴 거에요	That'll take a few days
일 주일 걸릴 거에요	That'll take a week
차가 완전히 망가졌네요	Your car is a write-off
고칠 수 없어요	It can't be repaired
차/오토바이/모터 자전거/ 자전거를... 시에 찾으러 오세요	The car/motorcycle/moped/ bicycle will be ready at ...o'clock

5.7 Renting a car

● **To rent a car**, a driver should have more than one year's experience, an international driver's license, a passport and should be over 21 years old.

I'd like to rent a...
...를 빌리고 싶은데요
...reul bil li go si peun de yo

Do I need a (special)
license for that?
이걸 쓰려면 (특수) 면허증이
필요한가요?
**I geol sseu ryeo myeon (teuk su)
myeon heo jjeung-i pi ryo han ga yo?**

I'd like to rent the...for...
...를...에 쓰려고 빌리고 싶어요
...reul...e sseu ryeo go bil li go si peo yo

the...for a day
...를 하루 빌리고 싶어요
...reul ha ru bil li go si peo yo

the...for two days
...를 이틀간 빌리고 싶어요
...reul i teul gan bil li go si peo yo

How much is that
per day week?
하루/일 주일에 얼마인가요?
Ha ru e/il ju i re eol ma i n-ga yo?

How much is the
deposit?
예치금은 얼마인가요?
Ye chi geu meun eol ma i n-ga yo?

Could I have a receipt
for the deposit?
예치금 영수증을 받을 수 있나요?
**Ye chi geum yeong su jeung-eul
ba deul su in na yo?**

The parts of a motorcycle/bicycle

(the diagram shows the numbered parts)

1	rear light	미등	mi deung
2	rear wheel	뒷 바퀴	dwit ba kwi
3	(luggage) carrier	바구니	ba gu ni
4	fork	포크 케이블	po keu ke i beul
5	bell	벨	bel
	inner tube	튜브	tyu beu
	tire	타이어	ta i eo
6	peddle crank	페달축	pe dal chuk
7	gear change	기어	gi eo
	wire	와이어	wa i eo
	generator	제너레이터	ge neo re i teo
	frame	프레임	p re im
8	wheel guard	휠 가드	hwil ga deu
9	chain	체인	che in
	chain guard	체인 가드	che in ga deu
	odometer	주행계	ju haeng-gye
	child's seat	아동용 의자	a dong-yong ui ja
10	headlight	전조등	jeon jo deung
	bulb	벌브	beol b
11	pedal	페달	pe dal
12	pump	펌프	peom peu
13	reflector	반사경	ban sa gyeong
14	brake shoe	브레이크	b re i keu
15	brake cable	브레이크 케이블	b re i keu ke i beul
16	anti-theft device	도난 방지 장치	do nan bang ji jang chi
17	carrier straps	소품걸이	so pum geo li
	tachometer	스피드 미터	seu pi deu mi teo
18	spoke	스포크	seu po keu
19	mudguard	진흙받이	jin heuk ba ji
20	handlebar	손잡이	son ja bi
21	chain wheel	체인	che in
	toe clip	발 고정기	bal go jeoong-gi
22	crank axle	크랭크	keu raeng keu
	drum brake	드럼 브레이크	deu reom beu re i keu
23	rim	틀	teul
24	valve	밸브	bael beu
25	gear cable	기어 케이블	gi eo ke i beul
26	fork	포크 케이블	po keu ke i beul
27	front wheel	앞 바퀴	ap ba kwi
28	seat	의자	ui ja

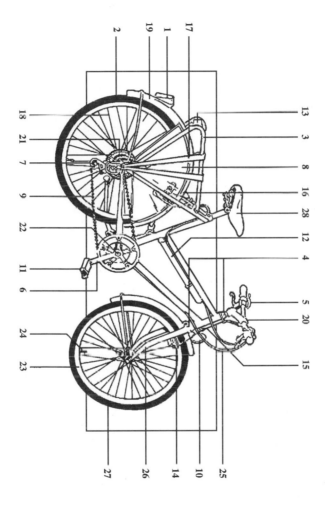

How much is the surcharge per kilometer?	킬로 당 추가 요금은 얼마인가요? **Kil lo dang chu ga yo geu meun eol ma i n-ga yo?**
Does that include gas?	기름도 포함하고 있나요? **Gi reum do po ham ha go in na yo?**
Does that include insurance?	보험도 되나요? **Bo heom do doe na yo?**
What time can I pick the...up?	...를 몇 시에 가지러 오면 되나요? **...reul myeot si e ga ji reo o myeon doe na yo?**
When does it have to be back?	언제까지 반납해야 하나요? **Eon je kka ji ban nap hae ya ha na yo?**
Where's the gas tank?	기름탱크는 어디에 있나요? **Gi reum taen keu neun eo di e in na yo?**
What sort of fuel does it take?	어떤 연료를 쓰나요? **Eo tteon yeol lyo reul sseu na yo?**

5.8 Hitchhiking

● **Hitchhiking** is very rare in Korea. Getting a ride from a stranger may be difficult, but these are some common directions and courtesies.

Where are you heading?	어디 가요? **Eo di ga yo?**
Can you give me a lift?	태워 주시겠어요? **Tae wo ju si ge sseo yo?**
Can my friend come too?	제 친구도 타도 돼요? **Je chin-gu do ta do dwae yo?**
I'd like to go to...	...에 가고 싶은데요 **...e ga go si peun deo yo**
Is that on the way to...?	...로 가는 길이세요? **...ro ga neun gi ri se yo?**
Could you drop me off...?	...에 좀 내려 주세요 **...e jom nae ryeo ju se yo**
Could you drop me off here?	여기서 좀 내려주세요 **Yeo gi seo jom nae ryeo ju se yo**

Could you drop me off at the entrance to the highway?	고속도로 진입할 때 좀 내려주세요 **Go sok do ro jin nip hal ttae jom nae ryeo ju se yo**
Could you drop me off in the center?	센터에 좀 내려주세요 **Sen teo e jom nae ryeo ju se yo**
Could you drop me off at the next intersection?	다음 교차로에서 좀 세워 주세요 **Da eum gyo cha ro e seo jom se wo ju se yo**
Could you stop here, please?	여기에 좀 세워 주세요 **Yeo gi e jom se wo ju se yo**
I'd like to get out here	여기서 내려 주세요 **Yeo gi e nae ryeo ju se yo**
Thanks for the lift	태위 주서서 감사합니다 **Tae wo ju syeo seo gam sa ham mi da**

6 Arrival and Departure

6. Arrival and Departure

● **There are more than ten subway lines** in Seoul, each indicated by a different color. They link the farthest parts of Seoul and its satellite cities and transfers between lines may be made at various stations. Trains operate at intervals of 2.5 to 3 minutes during the morning and evening rush hours, and at intervals of 4 to 6 minutes during the rest of the day.

There are three kinds of urban buses running in Seoul: City, City Express and Deluxe Express. The City Express buses (*jwaseok*) are more comfortable than City buses (*ilban*). There is a further type of bus (*maeul*) that is a kind of a shuttle bus: it runs over short distances in residential areas that lack convenient transportation such as the subway or regular buses. Usually these buses are smaller and cheaper than the normal buses. Since the transportation card is not yet valid for these buses, fares have to be paid in cash.

You may get assistance from your hotel front desk to find out where the bus stops are and which number you need to take. You may also contact the Bus Route Information Center.

6.1 General

(…시)…행 기차가…분까지(정도) 연착되고 있습니다	The [time] train to…has been delayed by (about)…minutes
지금…행 기차가 승강장에 도착하고 있습 니다	The train to…is now arriving
…발 기차가 승강장에 들어오고 있습니다	The train from…is now arriving
다음 역은 … 입니다.	The next station is…

Where does this train go to?	이 기차는 어디로 가나요? I gi cha neun eo di ro ga na yo?
Does this boat go to…?	이 배는 …로 가나요? I bae neun …ro ga na yo?

Can I take this bus to...?	...로 가려면 이 버스를 타면 되나요? **...ro ga ryeo myeon i beo seu reul ta myeon doe na yo?**
Does this train stop at...?	이 기차가 ...에 서나요? **I gi cha ga ...e seo na yo?**
Is this seat taken/free/ reserved?	이 자리에 누가 있습니까?/빈자리 입니까?/예약된 자리인가요? **I ja ri e nu ga i sseum mi kka?/bin ja ri im mi kka?/yeo yak doen ja ri in-ga yo?**
I've reserved...	...를 예약했는데요. **...reul ye yak haen neun deo yo**
Could you tell me where I have to get off for...?	...로 가려면 어디에서 내리면 되나요? **...ro ga yeo myeon eo di e seo nae ri myeon doe na yo?**
Could you let me know when we get to...?	...에 도착하면 알려 주세요. **...e do chak ha myeon al lyeo ju se yo**
Could you stop at the next stop, please?	다음 역에 세워 주세요 **Da eum nyeo ge se wo ju se yo**
Where are we?	여기가 어딘가요? **Yeo gi ga eo din-ga yo?**
Do I have to get off here?	여기에서 내려야 하나요? **Yeo gi e seo nae ryeo ya ha na yo?**
Have we already passed...?	벌써...를 지나쳤어요? **Beol sseo ...reul ji na chyeo sseo yo?**
How long have I been asleep?	제가 잠을 얼마나 잤나요? **Je ga ja meul eol ma na jan na yo?**
How long does the train stop here?	기차가 여기에 얼마동안 멈출까요? **Gi cha ga yeo gi e eol ma ttong-an meom chul kka yo?**
Can I come back on the same ticket?	돌아갈 때 같은 표를 쓰면 되나요? **Do ra gal ttae ga teun pyo reul sseu myeon doe na yo?**
Can I change on this ticket?	이 표로 갈아탈 수 있나요? **I pyo ro ga ra tal su in na yo?**
How long is this ticket valid for?	이 표는 유효기간이 얼마동안 인가요? **I pyo neun yu hyo gi ga ni eol ma ttong-an in-ga yo?**

| How much is the extra fare for the high speed train? | 고속열차를 타려면 추가 비용이 얼마인가요? |
| | **Go song.yeol cha reul ta ryeo myeon chu ga bi yong-i eol ma in-ga yo?** |

6.2 Customs

여권 주세요	Your passport, please
영주권 보여 주세요	Your green card, please
자동차 등록서류 주세요	Your vehicle documents, please
사증/비자 보여주세요.	Your visa, please
어디로 가나요?	Where are you going?
얼마동안 머물 계획인가요?	How long are you planning to stay?
신고할 것이 있습니까?.	Do you have anything to declare?
이깃 열어주세요	Open this, please

My children are entered on this passport	우리 아이들은 이 여권으로 들어왔어요
	Uri a i deu reun i yeo kkwo neu ro deu reo wa sseo yo
I'm traveling through...	...로 여행할 거에요
	...ro yeo haeng-hal geo ye yo
I'm going on vacation to...	...로 휴가 갈 거에요
	...ro hu ga gal geo ye yo
I'm on a business trip	출장 중이에요
	Chul jjang jung-i e yo
I don't know how long I'll be staying	ㅣ얼마나 머무를지 아직 모르겠어요
	Eol ma na meo mu reul jji a jik mo reu ge sseo yo
I'll be staying here for a weekend	여기에 주말동안 머물 거에요
	Yeo gi e ju mal dong-an meo mul geo e yo
I'll be staying here for a few days	여기에 며칠동안 머물 거에요
	Yeo gi e myeo chil dong-an meo mul geo e yo

I'll be staying here a week	여기 일 주일 머물 거에요
	Yeo gie il ju il meo mul geo e yo
I'll be staying here for two weeks	여기 이 주일 머물 거에요
	Yeo gie i ju il meo mul geo e yo
I've got nothing to declare	신고할 것이 없어요
	Sin-go hal geo si eop sseo yo
I have...	...가 있어요
	...ga i sseo yo
a carton of cigarettes	담배 한 보루
	dam bae han bo ru
a bottle of...	...한 병
	...han byeong
some souvenirs	기념품
	gi nyeom pum
These are personal items	이건 개인 물건이에요
	I geon gae in mul geo ni e yo
These are not new	이건 새 것이 아니에요
	I geon sae geo si a ni e yo
Here's the receipt	영수증 여기 있어요
	Yeong su jeung yeo gi i sseo yo
This is for private use	이건 개인 용도로 산 거에요
	I geon gae in yong do ro san geo e yo
How much import duty do I have to pay?	수입관세를 얼마나 내야 하나요?
	Su ip gwan se reul eol ma na nae ya ha na yo?
May I go now?	이제 가도 되나요?
	I je ga do doe na yo?

6.3 Luggage

Porter!	여기요!
	Yeo gi yo!
luggage to...?	이 짐을...로 옮겨주세요
	I ji meul...ro om gyeo ju se yo
How much do I owe you?	얼마를 드리면 되나요?
	Eol ma reul deu ri meun doe na yo?

Where can I find a cart?	카트는 어디에 있나요? **Ka teu neun eo di e in na yo?**
Could you store this luggage for me?	이 짐을 좀 보관해 주세요 **I ji meul jom bo gwan hae ju se yo**
Where are the luggage lockers?	물품 보관소는 어디에 있나요? **Mul pum bo gwan so neun eo di e in na yo?**
I can't get the locker open	보관함을 열 수가 없어요 **Bo gwan ha meul yeol su ga eop seo yo**
How much is it per item per day?	하루에 한 품목 당 얼마인가요? **Ha ru e han pum mok-dang eol ma in ga yo?**
This is not my bag/ suit case	이건 제 가방/서류 가방이 아닌데요 **I geon je ga bang/seo ryu ga bang-i a nin de yo**
There's one item/bag/ suitcase missing	한 개/가방/서류 가방이 없어졌어요 **Han gae/ga bang/seo ryu ga bang-i eop seo jyeo sseo yo**
My suitcase is damaged	제 서류 가방에 손상이 생겼어요 **Je seo ryu ga bang-e son sang-i saeng-gyeo sseo yo**

6.4 Questions to passengers

Ticket types

일등석/이등석	First/second class
편도/왕복	Single/return
흡연/금연	Smoking/non-smoking
창가 쪽 좌석	Window seat
앞 쪽/뒤쪽	Front/back (of train)
좌석/침대	Seat/berth
위/가운데/아래	Top/middle/bottom
일반석/일등석	Economy/first class
선실/좌석	Cabin/seat

| 일인용/이인용 | Single/double |
| 몇 명이세요? | How many are traveling? |

Destination

어디로 가나요?	Where are you traveling?
언제 떠나나요?	When are you leaving?
...는...시에 출발합니다	Your...leaves at...
...를 바꿔야 해요	You have to change
...에서 내려야 해요	You have to get off at...
...를 통해서/경유해서 가야 해요	You have to go via....
...(일)에 출발해요	The outward journey is on...
...(일)에 도착해요	The return journey is on...
...시까지는 타야/탑승해야	You have to be on board
합니다	by....(o'clock)

Inside the vehicle

표 주세요	Tickets, please
예약(표) 주세요	Your reservation, please
여권 주세요	Your passport, please
다른 자리에 앉으셨어요	You're in the wrong seat
뭔가 실수를 한 것 같은데요/...	You have made a mistake/
를 잘 못 한 것 같은데요	You are in the wrong...
여기는 예약이 된 자리예요	This seat is reserved
추가 비용을 내야 해요	You'll have to pay extra
...가...분 연착되고 있습니다	The...has been delayed by...
	minutes

6.5 Tickets

Where can I...? | ...는 어디에서 하면 되나요?
...neun eo di e seo ha myeon doe na yo?

- buy a ticket?	표는 어디에서 팔아요? pyo neun eo di e seo pa ra yo?
- reserve a seat?	좌석은 어디에서 예약하면 되나요? jwa seo geun eo di e seo ye yak ha myeon doe na yo?
- reserve a flight?	비행기 표는 어디에서 예약하면 되나요? bi haeng-gi pyo neun eo di e seo ye yak ha myeon doe na yo?
Could I have...for...please?	...행...를 주세요 ...haeng ...reul ju se yo
A single to...please	...행 편도 한 장 주세요 ...haeng pyeon do han jang ju se yo
A return ticket, please	왕복 한 장 주세요 Wang bok han jang ju se yo
first class	일등석 il tteung seok
second class	이등석 il tteung seok
economy class	일반석 il ban seok
I'd like to reserve a seat/ berth/cabin	좌석/침대/선실을 예약하고 싶은데요 Jwa seok/chim dae/seon sil reul ye yak ha go si peun de yo
I'd like to reserve a top/ middle/bottom berth in the sleeping car	침니차 위/가운데/아래 침대를 예약하고 싶은데요 Chim dae cha wi/ga un de/a rae chim dae reul ye yak ha go si peun de yo
smoking/non-smoking	흡연/금연 heu byeon/geu myeon
by the window	창가 쪽 chang-ga jjok
single/double	일인석/이인석 i rin seok/i in seok
at the front/back	앞 쪽/뒤쪽 ap jjok/dwi jjok

There are...of us	...명 있어요 **...myeong i sseo yo**
We have a car	차가 있어요 **Cha ga i sseo yo**
We have a trailer	트레일러가 있어요 **Teu re il leo ga i sseo yo**
We have...bicycles	자전거...대를 가지고 있어요 **Ja jeon-geo...dae reul ga ji go i sseo yo**
Do you have a...	...가 있나요? **...ga in na yo?**
- weekly travel card?	주 정기권 있어요? **ju jeong-gi kkwon i sseo yo**
- monthly season ticket?	월 정기권 있어요? **wol jeong-gi kkwon i sseo yo?**
Where's...?	...는 어디 있나요? **...neun eo di in na yo?**
Where's the information desk?	안내소는 어디에 있나요? **An nae so neun eo di e in na yo?**

 Information

Where can I find a schedule?	운행시간표는 어디 있나요? **Un haeng si gan pyo neun eo di in na yo?**
Where's the...desk?	...소는 어디 있나요? **...so neun eo di in na yo?**
Do you have a city map with the bus/the subway routes on it?	버스/지하철 노선 지도가 있나요? **Beo seu/ji ha cheol no seon ji do ga in na yo?**
Do you have a schedule?	운행시간표 가지고 있나요? **Un haeng si gan pyo ga ji go in na yo?**
Will I get my money back?	환불해 주나요? **Hwan bul hae ju na yo?**
I'd like to go to...	...에 가고 싶은데요 **...e ga go si peun de yo**

I'd like to confirm/cancel/ change my reservation for/trip to...	...행 예약을 확인/취소/변경하고 싶은데요 **...haeng ye ya geul hwa gin/chwi so/ byeon-gyeong ha go si peun de yo**
What is the quickest way to get there?	거기까지 가는 제일 빠른 길이 어딘가요? **Geo gi kka ji ga neun je il ppa reun gi ri eo din-ga yo?**
How much is a single/ return to...?	...행 편도/왕복표 값은 얼마예요? **...haeng pyeon do/wang bok pyo gap seun eol ma ye yo?**
Do I have to pay extra?	추가 비용을 내야 하나요? **Chu ga bi yong-eul nae ya ha na yo?**
Can I break my journey with this ticket?	이 표로 중간에 내렸다 다시 탈 수 있어요? **I pyo ro jung-ga ne nae ryeot da da si tal su i sseo yo?**
How much luggage am I allowed?	짐은 얼마까지 돼요? **Ji meun eol ma kka ji dwae yo?**
Is this a direct train?	이건 직행인가요? **I geon jik haeng in-ga yo?**
Do I have to change?	갈아 타야 돼요? **Ga ra ta ya dwae yo?**
Where?	어디에서요? **Eo di e seo yo?**
Does the plane stop anywhere?	비행기가 어디에 들르나요? **Bi haeng-gi ga eo di e deul leu na yo?**
Will there be any stopovers?	어디 경유해서 가요? **Eo di gyeong-yu hae seo ga yo?**
Does the boat stop at any other ports on the way?	이 배는 가다가 어디 들러요? **I bae neun ga da ga eo di deul leo yo?**
Does the train/bus stop at...?	이 기차/버스가...에 서요? **I gi cha/beo seu ga ...e seo yo?**
Where do I get off?	어디서 내려요? **Eo di seo nae ryeo yo?**
Is there a connection to...?	...로 가는 연결편이 있나요? **...ro ga neun yeon-gye pyeo ni in na yo?**

How long do I have to wait?	얼마나 기다려야 해요? **Eol ma na gi da ryeo ya hae yo?**
When does...leave?	...가 언제 떠나요? **...ga eon je tteo na yo?**
What time does the first/ next/last...leave?	첫/다음/마지막...는 몇 시에 떠나요? **Cheot/da eum/ma ji mak ...neun myeot si e tteo na yo?**
How long does...take?	...는 얼마나 걸리나요? **...neun eol ma na geo lli na yo?**
What time does it arrive in...?	...에 몇 시에 도착해요? **...e myeot si e do chak hae yo?**
Where does the...to...leave from?	... 행...가 어디서 출발해요? **...haeng...ga eo di seo chul bar hae yo?**
Is this the train/ bus...to...?	...로 가는 기차/버스 있나요? **...ro ga neun gi cha/beo seu in na yo?**

6.7 Airplanes

● **On arrival** at one of Korea's many international and domestic airports, you will find the following signs:

체크 인 check-in	국제선 international	국내선 domestic flights
도착 arrivals	출발 departures	

6.8 Trains

● **Korea** is well-served by an extensive network of express and local trains operated by the Korean National Railroad. Special package tours are available for foreign travelers and prices vary for first class, standard class and sleeping cars.

6.9 Taxis

임대	빈 차	택시 승차장
for hire	not occupied	taxi stand

Taxi!
택시!
Taek si!

Could you get me a taxi, please?
택시 좀 불러 주세요
Taek si jom bul leo ju se yo

Where can I find a taxi around here?
이 근처 어디에서 택시를 잡을 수 있나요?
I geun cheo eo di e seo taek si reul ja beul su in na yo?

Could you take me to..., please?
...까지 데려다 주세요
...kka ji de ryeo da ju se yo

to this address
까지 갑니다
kka ji gam mi da

to the...hotel
...호텔까지 가요
...ho tel kka ji ga yo

to the town/city center
시내에 가 주세요
si nae e ga ju se yo

to the station
역에 갑니다
yeo ge gam mi da

to the airport, please
공항에 가요
gong hang-e ga yo

How much is the trip to...?
...까지 얼마에요?
...kka ji eol ma ye yo?

How far is it to...?
...까지 얼마나 먼가요?
...kka ji eol ma na meon-ga yo?

Could you turn on the meter, please?
미터기 올려 주세요
Mi teo gi ol lyeo ju se yo

I'm in a hurry
좀 급해요
Jom geup hae yo

Could you speed up/ slow down a little?
좀 더 빨리/천천히 가 주세요
Jom deo ppal li/cheon cheon hi ga ju se yo

Could you take a different route?	다른 길로 가 주세요
	Da reun gil lo ga ju se yo
I'd like to get out here, please	여기 세워 주세요
	Yeo gi se wo ju se yo
Go...	...갑시다
	...gap si da
You have to go...here	여기서...가야 해요
	Yeo gi seo...ga ya hae yo
Go straight ahead	앞으로 똑바로 가세요
	A peu ro ddok ba ro ga se yo
Turn left	좌회전이요
	Jwa hwoe jeo ni yo
Turn right	우회전이요
	U heo jeo ni yo
This is it/We're here	다 왔어요
	Da wa sseo yo
Could you wait a minute for me, please?	잠시만 기다려 주세요
	Jam si man gi da ryeo ju s eyo

7 A Place to Stay

7. A Place to Stay

7.1 General

얼마나 오래 계실 건가요?	How long will you be staying?
이 용지를 작성해 주세요	Fill out this form, please
여권 좀 보여주세요	Could I see your passport?
예치금이 필요해요	I'll need a deposit
선불로/미리 지불해야만 합니다	You'll have to pay in advance

My name is...
제 이름은... 입니다
Je i reu meun...im mi da

I've made a reservation
예약을 했어요
Ye ya geul hae sseo yo

How much is it per
night/week/month?
하룻밤/한 주/한 달에 얼마인가요?
Ha rut bam/han ju/han dar-e
eol ma in-ga yo?

We'll be staying at
least...nights/weeks
여기에 적어도...일/주 머물 거에요
Yeo gi e jeo geo do...chil/ju
meo mul kkeo e yo

We don't know yet
아직 잘 모르겠어요
A jik jal mo reu ge sseo yo

Do you allow pets?
애완동물도 허용되나요?
Ae wan dong mul do
heo yong doe na yo?

What time does the door
open/close?
몇 시에 문을 여세요/닫으세요?
Myeot si e mu neul yeo se yo/
da deu se yo?

Could you get me a taxi,
please?
택시를 불러 주세요
Taek si reul bul leo ju se yo

Is there any mail for me?
저한테 온 우편물 있나요?
Jeo han te on u pyeon mul in na yo?

7.2 Hotels/B&Bs/apartments/holiday rentals

Do you have a single/
double room available?

일인용/이인용 빈 방 있나요?
I rin yong/i in yong bin bang in na yo?

per person/per room

일인당/방 하나 당
i rin dang/bang ha na dang

Does that include
breakfast/lunch/dinner?

아침/점심/저녁 식사도 포함되나요?
A chim/jeom sim/jeo nyeok sik sa do
po ham doe na yo?

Could we have two
adjoining rooms?

붙어 있는 방으로 두 개 주세요
Bu teo in neun bang-eu ro du gae
ju se yo

with/without toilet/
bath/shower

화잠실/욕실/샤워실이 있는/없는
hwa jang sil/yok sil/sya wo si ri in neun/
eom neun

facing the street

길쪽으로 향하는
gil jjo geu ro hwang ha neun

at the back

뒤쪽에
dwi jjo ge

with/without sea view

바다 경치가 보이는/보이지 않는
ba da gyeong chi ga bo i neun/bo i ji
an neun

Is there...in the hotel?

호텔에...가 있나요?
Ho te re ...ga in na yo?

Is there an elevator in
the hotel?

호델에 승간기/엘리베이터가 있니요?
Ho te re seung-gang-gi/el li be i teo ga
in na yo?

Do you have room
service?

룸서비스 되나요?
Rum seo bi seu doe na yo?

Could I see the room?

방을 볼 수 있을까요?
Bang-eul bol su i sseul kka yo?

I'll take this room

이 방으로 할게요.
I bang-eu ro hal kke yo?

We don't like this one

이건 마음에 들지 않네요
I geon ma eu me deul ji an ne yo

Do you have a larger/
less expensive room?

좀 더 비싼/싼 방이 있나요?
Jom deo bi ssan/ssan bang-i in na yo?

What time's breakfast?	아침 식사는 몇 시 인가요?
	A chim sik sa neun myeot si-in-ga yo?
Where's the dining room?	식당은 어디에 있나요?
	Sik dang-eun eo di e in na yo?
Can I have breakfast in my room?	제 방에서 아침을 먹어도 되나요?
	Je bang-e seo a chi meul meo geo do doe na yo?
Where's the emergency exit/fire escape?	비상구/화재 대피구는 어디인가요?
	Bi sang-gu neun/hwa jae dae pi gu neun eo di-in-ga yo?
Where can I park my car safely?	차는 어디에 주차하면 되나요?
	Cha neun eo di e ju cha ha myeon doe na yo?
The key to room..., please	...호실 열쇠 주세요
	...ho sil yeol soe ju se yo
Could you put this in the safe, please?	이걸 보관해 주세요
	I geol bo gwan hae ju se yo
Could you wake me at...tomorrow?	내일...시에 깨워 주세요
	Nae il ...si e kkae wo ju se yo
Could you find a babysitter for me?	아이 봐 줄 사람을 찾아봐 주세요
	A i bwa jul sa ram rul cha ja bwa ju se yo
Could I have an extra blanket?	여분의 담요가 필요해요
	Yeo bu nui dam nyo ga pi ryo hae yo
What days do the cleaners come in?	청소하러 무슨 요일에 오나요?
	Cheong so ha reo mu seun yo i re o na yo?
When are the sheets/towels/dish towels changed?	시트/수건/행주는 언제 갈아주나요?
	Si teu/su geon/haeng ju neun eon je ga ra ju na yo?

화장실과 샤워실은 같은 층에/실내에 있습니다	The toilet and shower are on the same floor/in the room
이쪽으로 오세요	This way please
손님의 방은...층, ...호실입니다	Your room is on the...floor, number...

We can't sleep for
the noise

시끄러워서 잠을 잘 수가 없어요
**Si kkeu reo wo seo ja meul jal su ga
eop seo yo**

7.3 Complaints

Could you turn the radio
down, please?

라디오 소리를 좀 낮춰 주세요
Ra di o so ri reul jom na chwo ju se yo

We're out of toilet paper

화장실 휴지를 다 써 가요
Hwa jang sil hyu ji reul da sseo ga yo

There aren't any.../
there's not enough...

...가 없어요./모자라요
...ga eop seo yo./mo ja ra yo

The bed linen's dirty

침대 요가 지저분해요
Chim dae yo ga ji jeo bun hae yo

The room hasn't been
cleaned

방이 깨끗하지가 않아요
Bang-i kkae kkeut ha ji ga a na yo

The kitchen is not clean

부엌이 깨끗하지 않아요
Bu eo gi kkae kkeut ha ji a na yo

The kitchen utensils are
dirty

부엌 용구가 지저분해요
Bu eok yong-gu ga ji jeo bun hae yo

The heating isn't
working

난방이 안 되요
Na bang-i an doe yo

There's no (hot) water/
electricity

(뜨거운) 물이 안 나와요/전기가
안 들어와요
**(Tteu geo un) mu ri an na wa yo/jeon-
gi ga an deu reo wa yo**

...doesn't work/is broken

...가 안 되요./고장 났어요
...ga an doe yo/go jang na sseo yo

Could you have that
seen to?

이것 손 봐주세요
I geot son bwa ju se yo

Could I have another
room/site?

다른 방/곳을 주세요
Da reun bang/go seul ju se yo

The bed creaks terribly

침대가 심하게 삐걱거려요
**Chim dae ga sim ha ge ppi geok-
geo ryeo yo**

The bed sags

침대가 내려 앉았어요.
Chim dae ga na ryeo an ja sseo yo

Could I have a board under the mattress?	매트리스 밑에 판을 대 주세요 **Mae teu ri seu mi te pa neul dae ju se yo**
It's too noisy	너무 시끄러워요 **Neo mu si kkeu reo wo yo**
There are a lot of insects/bugs	벌레가 너무 많아요 **Beol lae ga neo mu ma na yo**
This place is full of mosquitoes	여긴 모기가 너무 많아요 **Yeo gin mo gi ga neo mu ma na yo**
This place is full of cockroaches	여긴 바퀴벌레가 너무 많아요 **Yeo gin ba kwi beol lae ga neo mu ma na yo**

 **Departure**

See also 8.2 Settling the bill

I'm leaving tomorrow	내일 떠날 예정입니다 **Nae il tteo nal ye jeong-im mi da**
Could I pay my bill, please?	요금 계산하고 싶은데요 **Yo geum gye san ha go si peun de yo**
What time should we check out?	몇 시에 체크아웃 하면 되나요? **Myeot si e che keu a ut ha myeon doe na yo?**
Could I have my deposit/ passport back, please?	예치금/여권을 돌려 주세요 **Yeo chi geum/yeo kkwo neul dol lyeo ju se yo**
We're in a big hurry	지금 너무 급해요 **Ji geum neo mu geup hae yo**
Could you forward my mail to this address?	제 우편물을 이 주소로 보내주세요 **Je u pyeon mu reul i ju so ro bo nae ju se yo**
Could we leave our luggage here until we leave?	떠날 때까지 짐을 여기 둬도 되나요? **Tteo nal ddae kka ji ji meul yeo gi dwo do doe na yo?**
Thanks for your hospitality	친절하게 대해 주셔서 감사합니다 **Chin jeol ha ge dae hae ju syeo seo gam sa ham mi da**

7.5 Camping/backpacking

See the diagram on page 97

야영지를 직접 고를 수 있어요	You can pick your own site
야영지를 배정할 거에요	You'll be allocated a site
이게 야영지 번호 입니다	This is your site number
이것을 손님 차에 단단히 붙여 주세요	Please stick this firmly to your car
이 카드를 잃어버리면 안 됩니다	You must not lose this card

Where's the manager?
메니저는 어디에 있나요?
Mae ni jeo neon eo di e in na yo?

Are we allowed to camp here?
여기에 야영해도 되나요?
Yeo gi e ya yeong hae do doe na yo?

There are...of us and we have...tents
...명과 텐트...개가 있습니다
...myeong-gwa ten teu ...gae ga it sseum mi da

Can we pick our own site?
우리가 야영지를 직접 골라도 되나요?
U ri ga ya yeong-ji reul jik jeop gol la do doe na yo?

Do you have a quiet spot for us?
좀 조용한 곳을 찾는데요
Jom jo yong han go seul chan neun de yo

Do you have any other sites available?
다른 데에 빈 곳이 있나요?
Da reun de e bin go si in na yo?

It's too windy/sunny/shady here
여긴 바람이 너무 불어요/햇볕이 심해요/그늘이 져요
Yeo gin ba ra mi neo mu bu reo yo/ haet byeo chi sim hae yo/geu neu ri jyeo yo

It's too crowded here
여긴 너무 복잡해요
Yeo gin neo mu bok jap hae yo

The ground's too hard/uneven
땅이 너무 단단해요./울퉁불퉁해요
Ttang-i neo mu dan dan hae yo./ ul tung bul tung hae yo

A Place to Stay

7

95

Camping/backpacking equipment
(the diagram shows the numbered parts)

A Place to Stay

7

	luggage space	수화물 보관소	su hwa mul bo gwan so
	can opener	병따개	byeong tta gae
	butane gas	부탄 가스	bu tan ga seu
	bottle	병	byeong
1	pannier	짐 바구니	jim bba gu ni
2	gas cooker	가스 요리기구	ga seu yo ri gi gu
3	hammer	망치	mang chi
	hammock	그물 침대	geu mul chim dae
4	gas can	가스 용기	ga seu yong-gi
	campfire	캠프파이어/모닥불	kaem p-pa i eo/mo dak bul
5	folding chair	접이 의자	jeo bi ui ja
6	ice pack	얼음 주머니	eo reum ju meo ni
	compass	나침반	na chim ban
	corkscrew	코르크 마개 뽑이	ko reu keu ma gae ppo bi
7	airbed	공기 침대	gong gi chim dae
8	airbed pump	공기침대 펌프	gong gi chim ae peom peu
9	awning	천막	cheon mak
10	sleeping bag	침낭	chim nang
11	saucepan	냄비/소스팬	naem bi/so seu paen
12	handle (pan)	손잡이 냄비	son ja bi naem bi
	lighter	라이터/점화기	ra i teo/jeom hwa gi
13	backpack	배낭	bae nang
14	rope	로프	ro peu
15	storm lantern	전등	jeon deung
	camp bed	야영 침대	ya yeong chim dae
	table	탁자	tak ja
16	tent	텐트/천막	ten teu/chun mak
17	tent peg	천막 말뚝	chun mak mal ttuk
18	tent pole	천막 기둥	chun mak gi dung
	thermos	보온병	bo on ppyeong
19	water bottle	물병	mul ppyeong
	clothes pin	빨래집게	ppal lae jip ge
	clothes line	빨래 줄	ppal lae jjul
	windbreak	바람 막이	ba ram-ma gi
20	flashlight	손전등	son jeon deung
	penknife	주머니칼	ju meo ni kal

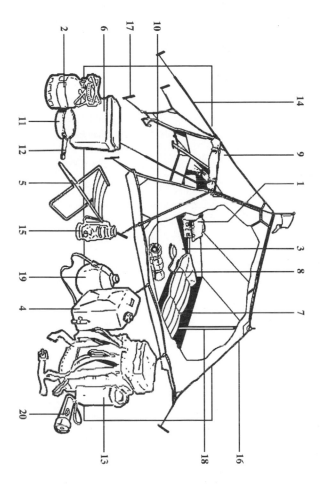

Do you have a level spot for the camper/trailer/folding trailer?	야영/이동주택/조립주택으로 사용할 수 있는 평평한 곳이 있나요? Ya yeong/i dong ju taek/ jo rip ju tae geu ro sa yong hal su in neun pyeong pyeong han go si in na yo?
Could we have adjoining sites?	붙어있는 곳으로 주세요 Bu teo in neun go seu ro ju se yo
How much is it per person/tent/car?	일인당/한 텐트 당/차 한대 당 얼마인가요? I rin dang/han ten teu dang/cha han dae dang eol ma in-ga yo?
Do you have chalets for hire?	임대 중인 별장이 있나요? Im dae jung.in byeol jjang-i in na yo?
Are there any...?	...가 있나요? ...ga in na yo?
Are there any hot showers?	온수가 나오는 샤워실이 있나요? On su ga na o neun sya wo si ri in na yo?
Are there any washing machines?	세탁기가 있나요? Se tak gi ga in na yo?
Is there a...on the site?	야영지에...가 있나요? Ya yeong-ji e...ga in na yo?
Is there a children's play area on the site?	야영지에 놀이터가 있나요? Ya yeong-ji e no ri teo ga in na yo?
Are there covered cooking facilities on the site?	야영지에 요리시설이 있나요? Ya yeong-ji e yo ri si seo ri in na yo?
Are we allowed to barbecue here?	바비큐 파티를 해도 되나요? Ba bi kyu pa ti reul hae do doe na yo?
Are there any power outlets?	전선 꽂을 데가 있어요? Jeon seon kko jeul de ga i sseo yo?
Is there drinking water?	식용수가 있나요? Si gyong su ga in na yo?
When's the garbage collected?	쓰레기는 언제 치워가나요? Sseu re gi neun eon je chi wo ga na yo?
Do you sell gas bottles (butane gas/ropane gas)?	가스통(부탄 가스/프로판 가스) 팔아요? Ga seu tong (bu tan ga seu/peu ro pan ga seu) pa ra yo?

8 Money matters

8. Money matters

8.1 Banks

Where can I find a bank around here?	은행이 이 근처 어디에 있어요? **Eun haeng-i i geun cheo eo di e i sseo yo?**
Where can I cash this traveler's check?	여행자 수표는 어디서 바꿀 수 있나요? **Yeo haeng ja su pyo neun eo di seo ba kkul su in na yo?**
Can I cash this...here?	여기서 이...바꿀 수 있어요? **Yeo gi seo i...ba kkul su i sseo yo?**
Can I withdraw money on my credit card here?	제 신용 카드로 현금인출이 되나요? **Je si nyong ka deu ro hyeon.geum in chu ri doe na yo?**
What's the minimum/ maximum amount?	최소/최대 한도액이 얼마예요? **Choe so/choe dae han do ae gi eol ma ye yo?**
Can I take out less than that?	그것보다 적게 인출도 되나요? **Geu geot bo da jeok ge in chul do doe na yo?**
I had some money cabled here	여기로 얼마 송금을 했어요 **Yeo gi ro eol ma song-geu meul hae sseo yo**
Has it arrived yet?	벌써 받았나요? **Beol sseo ba dan na yo?**
These are the details of my bank in the US	이건 미국에 있는 제 은행에 대한 세부 내용입니다 **I geon mi gu ge in neun je eun haeng-e dae han se bu nae yong.im mi da**
This is the number of my bank account	이게 제 은행 계좌 번호 입니다 **I ge je eun haeng gyeo jwa beon ho im mi da**
I'd like to change some money	돈을 좀 바꾸고 싶은데요 **Do neul jom ba kku go si peun de yo**
I'd like to change...Euros	유로를 바꾸고 싶은데요 **Eu ro reul ba kku go si peun de yo**

I'd like to change...dollars	달러를...로 바꾸고 싶은데요 **Dal leo reul ...ro ba kku go si peun de yo**
What's the exchange rate?	환율이 어떻게 되나요? **Hwan yu ri eo tteot ke doe na yo?**
Could you give me some small change with it?	이걸 잔돈으로 좀 바꿔주세요 **I geol jan do neu ro ba kkwo ju se yo**
This is not right	이건 맞지가 않는데요 **In geon mat ji ga an neun de yo**

여기 서명해 주세요	Sign here, please
이거 작성해 주세요	Fill this out, please
여권을 보여 주세요	Could I see your passport, please?
신분증을 보여 주세요	Could I see your identity card, please?
은행 카드를 보여 주세요	Could I see your bank card, please?

8.2 Settling the bill

Could you put it on my bill?	제 계산서에 포함시켜 주시겠어요? **Je gye san seo e po ham si kyeo ju si ge sseo yo?**
Is the tip included?	팁도 포함되나요? **Tip do po ham doe na yo?**
Can I pay by...?	...로 계산하고 싶은데요 **...ro gye san ha go si peun de yo**
Can I pay by credit card?	신용카드로 계산할게요 **Si nyong ka deu ro gye san hal kke yo**
Can I pay by traveler's check?	여행자 수표로 계산해도 되나요? **Yeo haeng ja su pyo ro gye san gae do doe na yo?**
Can I pay with foreign currency?	외국환으로 계산해도 되나요? **Oe guk hwa neu ro gye san hae do doe na yo?**

You've given me too much/you haven't given me enough change

거스름돈을 너무 많이 주셨어요./
잔돈을 덜 주셨네요

Geo seu reum do neul neo mu ma ni ju syeo sseo yo./jan do neul deol ju syeon ne yo

Could you check this again, please?

이거 다시 체크 해 주실래요?

I geo da si che keu hae ju sil lae yo?

Could I have a receipt, please?

영수증 주세요

Yeong su jeung ju se yo

I don't have enough money on me

돈이 좀 모자라는데요

Do ni jom mo ja ra neun de yo

This is for you

여기 있습니다

Yeo gi i sseum mi da

Keep the change

잔돈은 그냥 가지세요

Jan do neun geu nyang ga ji se yo

신용카드/여행자 수표/외국 돈은 받지 않 습니다.

We don't accept credit cards/ traveler's checks/ foreign currency

9 Mail, Phone and Internet

9. Mail, Phone and Internet

● **With the popularization** of the Internet, a number of Internet cafes and so-called 'PC rooms' have appeared everywhere in Korea. There, people enjoy surfing on the sea of information or playing games with other netizens around the world, along with snacks and music.

Post offices in Korea have been diversifying their business areas. A variety of banking services are now available at more than 3,000 post offices across the nation. They also operate mail order services and issue some civil affairs documents.

Mailing services are divided mainly into two kinds: speed delivery and ordinary delivery. Speed delivery mail arrives within 1-2 days for about double the postal rates, while ordinary mail arrives within 2-4 days.

Mail

우표 stamps	소포 parcels	우편환 money orders	국제 특송 우편 EMS

Where is...?	...어디에 있어요? ...eo di e i sseo yo?
Where is the nearest post office?	가까운 우체국 어디에 있어요? Ga kka un u che gu gi eo di e i sseo yo?
Where is the main post office	중앙 우체국이 어디에 있어요? Jung-ang u che gu gi eo di e i sseo yo?
Where is the nearest mail box?	가까운 우체통이 어디에 있어요? Ga kka un u che tong-i eo di e i sseo yo?
Which counter should I go to?	어느 창구로 가면 되나요? Eo neu chang-gu ro ga myeon doe na yo?
Which counter should I go to to send a fax?	팩스를 보내려면 어느 창구로 가면 되나요? Pak seu reul bo nae ryeo myeon eo neu chang-gu ro ga myeon doe na yo?

Which counter should I go to to change money?	돈을 바꾸려면 어느 창구로 가면 되나요? **Do neul ba kku ryeo myeon eo neu chang-gu ro ga myeon doe na yo?**
Which counter should I go to to send giro checks?	지로를 보내려면 어느 창구로 가면 되나요? **Ji ro reul bo nae ryeo myeon eo neu chang-gu ro ga myeon doe na yo?**
Which counter should I go to to wire a money order?	송금하려면 어느 창구로 가면 되나요? **Song-geum ha ryeo myeon eo neu chang-gu ro ga myeon doe na yo?**
Which counter should I go to for general delivery?	일반 우편은 어느 창구로 가면 되나요? **Il ban u pyeon bae da reun eo neu chang-gu ro ga myeon doe na yo?**
Is there any mail for me?	제게 온 우편있어요? **Je ge on u pyeon i sseo yo?**
My name's...	제 이름은... 입니다 **Je i reu meun...im mi da**

Stamps

What's the postage for ...to...?	...을...로 보내는데 얼마 들어요? **...eul...ro bo nae neun de eol ma deu reo yo?**
Are there enough stamps on it?	이 우표로 충분해요? **I u pyo ro chung bun hae yo?**
I'd like [value] [quantity] stamps	[value] 짜리 우표 [quantity] 장 주세요 **...jja ri u pyo...jang ju se yo**
I'd like to send this	이것을 보내려고 하는데요 **I geo seul bo nae ryeo go ha neun de yo**
I'd like to send this express	이걸 빠른우편으로 보내려고 하는데요 **I geol ppa reun u pyeo neu ro bo nae ryeo go ha neun de yo**
I'd like to send this by air mail	이걸 항공우편으로 보내려고 하는데요 **I geol hang-gong u pyeo neu ro bo nae ryeo go ha neun de yo**
I'd like to send this by registered mail	이걸 등기로 보내려고 하는데요 **I geol deung-gi ro bo nae ryeo go ha neun de yo**

EMS/fax

I'd like to EMS	국제 특송 우편을 보내려고 하는데요. **Guk je teuk song u pyeo neul** **bo nae ryeo go**
How much is it for …?	…로 보내는 데 얼마예요? **…ro bo na neun de eol ma ye yo?**
This is what I want to EMS	이것을 국제 특송 우편으로 보내려고 해요. **I geo seul guk je teuk song** **u pyeo neu ro**
Shall I fill out the form myself?	제가 써 넣어야 하나요? **Je ga sseo neo eo ya ha na yo?**
Can I make photocopies/ send a fax here?	여기서 복사/팩스 할 수 있어요? **Yeo gi seo bok sa/paek seu hal su** **i sseo yo?**
How much is it per page?	한 페이지에 얼마예요? **Han pe i ji e eol ma ye yo?**

9.2 Telephone

● **Direct international calls** can easily be made from public telephones using a phone card available from newspaper stands or from vending machines next to the telephone booths. Phone cards have a value of 2,000 or 3,000 Won. Dial 001 or 002 to get out of Korea, then the relevant country code (USA 1), city code and number.

Is there a phone booth around here?	근처에 공중전화 있어요? **Geun cheo-e gong jung jeon hwa** **i sseo yo?**
May I use your phone, please?	전화 좀 써도 될까요? **Jeon hwa jom sseo do doel kka yo?**
Do you have a phone directory?	전화 번호부 가지고 계세요? **Jeon hwa beon ho bu ga ji go** **gye se yo?**
Where can I get a phone card?	전화카드를 어디서 사나요? **Jeon hwa ka deu reul eo di seo** **sa na yo?**

| Could you give me...? | ...좀 가르쳐 주세요 |
| | **...jom ga reu cheo ju se yo** |

| Could you give me the number for international directory assistance? | 국제전화 안내번호를 좀 가르쳐 주세요 |
| | **Guk je jeon hwa an nae beon ho reul jom ga reu cheo ju se yo** |

| Could you give me the number of room...? | ...실 전화 번호를 좀 가르쳐 주세요 |
| | **...sil jeon hwa beon ho reul jom ga reu cheo ju se yo** |

| Could you give me the international access code? | 국제자동전화 식별번호를 좀 가르쳐 주세요 |
| | **Guk je ja dong jeon hwa sik byeol beon ho reul jom ga reu cheo ju se yo** |

| Could you give me the country code? | 국가 번호를 좀 가르쳐 주세요 |
| | **Guk ka beon ho reul jom ga reu cheo ju se yo** |

| Could you give me the area code? | 지역 번호를 좀 가르쳐 주세요 |
| | **Ji yeok beon ho reul jom ga reu cheo ju se yo** |

| Could you give me the number of [subscriber]...? | ...의 번호를 좀 가르쳐 주세요 |
| | **...ui beon ho reul jom ga reu cheo ju se yo** |

| Could you check if this number's correct? | 번호가 맞는 지 확인 좀 해 주세요 |
| | **Beon ho ga man neun ji hwa gin jom hae ju se yo** |

| Can I dial international direct? | 국제 직통 전화를 할 수 있나요? |
| | **Guk je jik tong jeon hwa reul hal su in na yo?** |

| Do I have to go through the switchboard? | 교환을 불러야 되나요? |
| | **Gyo hwa neul bul leo ya doe na yo?** |

| Do I have to dial '0' first? | 0 번을 먼저 눌러야 하나요? |
| | **Yeong beo neul meon jeo nul leo ya ha na yo?** |

| Do I have to reserve my calls? | 전화기록을 남겨둬야 하나요? |
| | **Jeon hwa gi ro geul nam gyeo dwo ya ha na yo?** |

| Could you dial this number for me, please? | 이 번호로 전화 좀 해 주실 수 있어요? |
| | **I beon ho ro jeon hwa jom hae ju sil su i sseo yo?** |

Could you put me through to extension..., please?
...번으로 연결해 주세요
...beo neu ro yeon gyeol hae ju se yo

I'd like to place a collect call to...
...에게 콜렉트 콜을 하려고 해요
...e ge kol lek t ko reul ha ryeo go hae yo

What's the charge per minute?
일 분에 얼마예요?
Il bu ne eol ma ye yo?

Have there been any calls for me?
제게 전화 온 거 있어요?
Je ge jeon hwa on geo i sseo yo?

The conversation

Hello, this is...
여보세요, ...입니다
Yeo bo se yo, ...im mi da

Who is this, please?
누구세요?
Nu gu se yo?

Is this...?
...이세요?
...i se yo?

I'm sorry, I've dialed the wrong number
죄송합니다, 잘 못 걸었어요.
Joe song.ham mi da, jal mot geo reo sseo yo

I can't hear you
잘 안 들리는 데요
Jal an deul li neun de yo

I'd like to speak to...
...좀 바꿔 주세요
...jom ba kkwo ju se yo

Is there anybody who speaks English?
영어를 할 줄 아는 분이 계세요?
Yeong eo reul hal ju ra neun bu ni gye se yo?

Extension..., please
...번으로 연결해 주세요
...beo neu ro yeon gyeol hae ju se yo

Could you ask him/her to call me back?
에게 전화해 달라고 전해주세요
Ege jeon hwa hae dal la go jeon hae ju se yo

My name's...
제 이름은 ... 입니다
Je i reu meun ... im mi da

My number's...
제 전화번호는...입니다
Je jeon hwa beon ho neun ... im mi da

Could you tell him/her I called?	제가 전화했다고 전해주세요 Je ga jeon hwa haet da go jeon hae ju se yo
I'll call him/her back tomorrow	내일 다시 전화할게요 Nae il da si jeon hwa hal ke yo

전화가 왔었습니다	There's a phone call for you
0 번을 먼저 누르세요	You have to dial '0' first
잠깐 기다리세요	One moment, please
응답이 없습니다	There's no answer
통화 중입니다	The line's busy
기다리시겠어요?	Do you want to hold?
연결 중입니다	Connecting you
잘 못 거셨습니다	You've got a wrong number
자리에 없습니다	He's/she's not here right now
잠시 후 돌아오실 겁니다	He'll/she'll be back later
...의 자동 응답기입니다	This is the answering machine of...

Mobile Phone

It's fast because it's a 4G smart phone.	4G 스마트폰이라 속도가 아주 빨라요. Four-G smart phone-ira sok do ga a ju ppal la yo.
My smart phone/I-phone has broken down.	제 스마트폰이/아이폰이 고장 났어요. Je smart phone-i/i-phone-i go jang na seo yo.
Please send me a text message.	문자 메시지 남겨 주세요. Mun ja me si ji nam gyeo ju se yo.
I will send you a text message.	문자 메시지 남길게요. Mun ja me si ji nam gil ge yo.
The (phone) connection is not good; it keeps being cut off.	(전화) 연결이 잘 안돼요. 자꾸 끊어져요. (Jeon hwa) yeong yeol-i jal an dwae yo. Ja kku kkeu neo jyeo yo.

 **Internet**

I cannot get on the Internet.	인터넷 연결이 안 돼요. **In ter net yeon gyeol-i an dwae yo.**
You can find it on Google.com/Naver.com.	구글로/네이버로 찾으면 나와요. **Google-ro/Naver-ro cha jeu myeon na wa yo.**
Do you have a wireless connection here?	여기 무선 인터넷 돼요? **Yeo gi mu seon In ter net dwae yo?**
Do I need a password to connect to the Internet?	인터넷 접속하려면 암호가 필요해요? **In ter net jeob sok ha ryeo myeon am ho ga pi ryo hae yo?**
The Internet is very fast/slow.	인터넷이 아주 빨라요/느려요. **In ter net-si a ju ppal la yo/neu ryeo yo.**

Social Media

Do you do Facebook?	페이스북 하세요? **Facebook ha se yo?**
Do you do Cyworld?	싸이월드 하세요? **Cyworld ha se yo?**
Do you tweet?	트위터 하세요? **Tweeter ha se yo?**
What is your blog address?	블로그 주소가 어떻게 돼요 **Blog ju so ga eo tteo ke dwae yo**
I saved my (digital) photos in my computer.	사진을 컴퓨터에 저장했어요. **Sa ji neul com pu ter-e jeo jang hae seo yo.**
I will email you these photos.	사진을 이메일로 보내 줄게요. **Sa ji neul email-ro bo nae jul ge yo.**

10 Shopping

10. Shopping

● **Most shops** in Korea are open for long hours. Major department stores are open from 10:30 a.m. until 8:00 p.m. including Sundays, but smaller shops are usually open until late evening every day. There are also 24-hour convenience stores available in major cities. You can converse in English in the shopping arcades of major hotels and certainly in Itaewon Market, which is located in Southern Seoul. Shops in Namdaemun Market and Dongdaemun Market in Seoul offer a variety of goods at bargain prices. There are 24-hour shops in Seoul, especially in the main shopping belts.

식품점 grocery shop	시계점 watches and clocks	모피전문점 furrier

빨래방
coin-operated
  laundry
	등산장비점
	camping supplies
	  shop
		가전제품
		household
		  appliances

사탕/케이크 전문점
confectioners/
  cake shop
	이불가게
	household linen
	  shop
		청과물상
		fruit and
		  vegetable shop

이발관 barbers	가구점 furniture shop	꽃집 florist
서점 book shop	중고상 second-hand shop	생선가게 fishmonger
장난감가게 toy shop	안경점 optician	닭 파는 집 poultry shop
인조 보석 costume jewelry	옷가게 clothing shop	청과물상 greengrocer
빵집 baker's shop, bakery	정육점 butcher's shop	향수전문점 perfumery

악기점
musical instrument
  shop
	유제품가게
	dairy (shop selling
	  dairy products)
		음반가게
		music shop (CDs,
		  tapes, etc)

신발가게 footwear	신문 가판대 newsstand	약국 pharmacy

철물점 hardware shop	아이스크림가게 ice cream shop	델리가게 delicatessen
구두수선 shoe repair	백화점 department store	세탁소 laundry
시장 market	미용실 hairdresser	보석상 jeweler
금세공 goldsmith	카메라점 camera shop	슈퍼마켓 supermarket
문구점 stationery shop	한의원 herbalist's shop	담배가게 tobacconist
포목점 fabric shop	운동구점 sporting goods	미용실 beauty salon
오토바이/자전거 수리점 motorbike/bicycle repairs	가죽전문점 leather goods	화원 nursery (plants)

10.1 Shopping conversations

Where can I get...?	...어디에 있어요? ...eo di e i sseo yo?
When is this shop open?	이 가게 몇 시까지 열어요? I ga ge myot si kka ji yeo reo yo?
Could you tell me where the ... department is?	...매장 어디에 있어요? ...mae jang eo di e i sseo yo?
Could you help me, please?	여기 좀 봐 주시겠어요? Yeo gi jom bwa ju si ge sseo yo?
I'm looking for ...	...찾고 있는데요 ...chat go in neun de yo
Do you sell English/ American newspapers?	영자 신문 있어요? Yeong ja sin mun i sseo yo?

도와 드릴까요?   Are you being served?

No, I'd like...	아뇨, ...고 싶어요
	A nyo, ...go si peo yo
I'm just looking, if that's all right	그냥 구경하는 중이에요
	Geu-nyang gu.gyeong ha neun jung.i e yo

또 필요하신 거 없으세요?　　Anything else?

Yes, I'd also like ...	네, ...도 주세요
	Ne, ...do ju se yo
No, thank you. That's all	아뇨, 괜찮아요. 그게 전부예요
	A nyo, gwaen cha na yo. geu ge jeon bu yeo yo.
Could you show me ...?	...좀 보여 주시겠어요?
	...jom bo yeo ju si ge sseo yo?
I'd prefer ...	...가 더 좋아요.
	...ga deo jo a yo
This is not what I'm looking for	이거 제가 찾는 거 아니예요
	I geo je ga chan neun geo a ni yeo yo
Thank you, I'll keep looking	감사합니다, 좀 더 구경하겠어요
	Gam sa ham ni da, jom deo gu gyeung ha ge sseo yo
Do you have something ...?	...거 있어요?
	...geo i sseo yo?
less expensive?	덜 비싼
	deol bi ssan
smaller?	더 작은
	deo ja geun
larger?	더 큰
	deo keun
I'll take this one	이거 사겠어요
	I geo sa ge sseo yo
Does it come with instructions?	설명서도 같이 있나요?
	Seol myeong seo do ga chi in na yo?

It's too expensive	너무 비싸요
	Neo mu bi ssa yo
I'll give you ...	...드리겠어요
	...deu ri ge sseo yo
Could you keep this for me?	이거 좀 보관해 주시겠어요?
	I geo jom bo gwan hae ju si ge sseo yo?
I'll come back for it later	나중에 가지러 오겠어요
	Na jung-e ga ji reo o ge sseo yo
Do you have a bag for me, please?	쇼핑백 하나 주시겠어요?
	Syo ping baek ha na ju si ge sseo yo?
Could you gift wrap it, please?	이거 선물포장 좀 해 주시겠어요?
	I geo seon mul po jang jom hae ju si ge sseo yo?

죄송합니다, 없습니다	I'm sorry, we don't have that
죄송합니다, 매진입니다	I'm sorry, we're sold out
죄송합니다, ... 까지는 안 들어옵니다	I'm sorry, it won't come back in until...
계산대에서 지불하세요	Please pay at the cash register
신용카드 안 받습니다	We don't accept credit cards
여행자 수표 안 받습니다	We don't accept traveler's checks
외국돈 안 받습니다	We don't accept foreign currency

10.2 Food

I'd like a hundred grams of ..., please	...백그람 주세요
	...baek geu ram ju se yo
I'd like half a kilo/five hundred grams of ...	...반 키로/...오백그람 주세요
	...ban ki ro/...o baek geu ram ju se yo
I'd like a kilo of...	...일키로 주세요
	...il ki ro ju se yo
Could you ... it for me, please?	...좀 주시겠어요?
	...jom ju si ge sseo yo?

slice it/cut it up for me, please?	썰어/잘라 주시겠어요? sseo reo/jal la ju si ge sseo yo?
grate it for me, please?	갈아 주시겠어요? ga ra ju si ge sseo yo?
Can I order it?	주문할 수 있어요? Ju mun hal su i sseo yo?
I'll pick it up tomorrow/ at ...	내일/... 시에 가지러 오겠어요 Nae il/... si e ga ji reo o ge sseo yo
Can you eat/drink this?	이거 먹을 수/마실 수 있어요? I geo meo geul su/ma sil su i sseo yo?
What's in it?	그 안에 뭐가 들었어요? Geu a ne mwo ga deu reo sseo yo?

10.3 Clothing and shoes

I saw something in the window	쇼 윈도우에서 뭘 좀 봤어요 Syo win do u e seo mwol jom bwa sseo yo
Shall I point it out?	가리켜 드릴까요? Ga ri kye deu ril kka yo?
I'd like something to go with this	이거하고 어울리는 걸 사고싶어요 I geo ha go eo ul li neun geol sa go si peo yo
Do you have shoes to match this?	이거하고 어울리는 신발 있어요? I geo ha go eo ul li neun sin bal i sseo yo?
I'm a size ... in the US	미국식으로 사이즈 ... 이에요 Mi guk si geu ro sa i jeu ... i e yo
Can I try this on?	이거 입어(clothing)/신어(shoes)봐도 돼요? I geo i beo(clothing)/si neo(shoes) bwa do dwae yo?
Where's the fitting room?	탈의실이 어디에 있어요? Ta ri si li eo di e i sseo yo?
It doesn't suit me	저에게 안 맞아요 Jeo e ge an ma ja yo

This is the right size	이게 맞는 사이즈예요 I ge man neun sa i jeu ye yo
It doesn't look good on me	저에게 안 어울려요 Jeo e ge an eo ul lyeo yo
Do you have this/these in …(size, color)?	이거 …로 있어요? I geo …ro i sseo yo?
The heels are too high/low	굽이 너무 높아요/낮아요 Gu bi neo mu no pa yo/na ja yo
Is this real leather?	이거 진짜 가죽이에요? I geo jin jja ga ju gi e yo?
I'm looking for a … for a …-year-old child	(age)… 살짜리 어린이용 (goods)…을/를 찾고 있어요 (Age)… sal jja ri eo ri ni yong (goods)…eul/reul chat go i sseo yo
I'd like a …	…을/를 사고 싶어요 …eul/reul sa go si peo yo
silk	실크 sil keu
cotton	면 myeon
woolen	울 ul
linen	린넨 rin nen
At what temperature should I wash it?	몇 도에 세탁해야 해요? Myeot do e se ta kae ya hae yo?
Will it shrink in the wash?	세탁 후에 줄이들이요? Se tak hu e ju reo deu reo yo?

손 세탁 Hand wash	다리지 마세요. Do not iron	탈수기로 짜지 마세요 Do not spin dry
드라이 클리닝 Dry clean	기계세탁 가능 Machine washable	뉘어서 말리세요 Lay flat

At the cobbler

Could you mend these shoes?	이 구두 좀 고쳐 주시겠어요? I gu du jom go chyeo ju si ge sseo yo?
Could you resole/reheel these shoes?	이 구두 밑창/굽 좀 갈아 주시겠어요? I gu du mit chang/gup jom ga ra ju si ge sseo yo?
When will they be ready?	언제 될까요? Eon je doel kka yo?
I'd like…, please	…좀 주세요 … jom ju se yo
a can of shoe polish	구두약 한 통 gu du yak han tong
a pair of shoelaces	구두끈 한 벌 gu du kkeun han beo

10.4 Photographs and electronic goods

I'd like batteries for this (digital) camera	이 카메라에 들어가는 배터리를 주세요 I ka me ra e deu reo ga neun bae teo ri reul ju se yo
I'd like a cartridge, please	카트릿지 하나 주세요 Ka teu rit ji ha na ju se yo
Two AA batteries, please	AA 배터리 두 개 주세요 AA bae teo ri du gae ju se yo
May I have a USB flash drive?	USB 메모리 카드 주세요 USB me mo ri ka deu ju se yo
Please scan the document and email it to me	그 문서를 스캔해서 보내 주세요 Geu mun seo reul scan-hae seo bo nae ju se yo
I-Pads are more popular than notebook computers	노트북보다 아이패드가 더 인기가 많아요 Notebook-bo da I-pad-ga deo in gi ga ma na yo
I attend a visual (virtual) conference on the computer	컴퓨터로 화상 회의를 해요 Computer-ro hwa sang hoe-ui-reul hae yo

Problems

Because the size of the
photo is too big,
I have to shrink it

사진의 용량이 너무 커서 크기를
줄여야 해요
Sa jin-ui yong nyang i neo mu keo seo
keu gi reul ju reo ya hae yo

Please delete the photo

사진을 삭제하세요
Sa ji neul sak je ha se yo

Please copy the photo

사진을 복사하세요
Sa ji neul bok sa ha se yo

Can you put in the
batteries for me, please?

배터리 좀 넣어 주시겠어요?
Bae teo ri jom neo eo ju si ge sseo yo?

Should I replace the
batteries?

밧데리를 갈아야 합니까?
Bat de ri reul ga ra ya ham ni kka?

Could you have a look at
my camera, please?

제 카메라 좀 봐 주시겠어요?
Je ka me ra jom bwa ju si ge sseo yo?

It's not working

작동이 안 돼요
Ja dong-i an dwae yo

The ... is broken

...이/가 고장났어요
...i/ga go jang na sseo yo

The camera memory
is full

메모리가 다 됐어요
Me mo ri ga da dwae seo yo

I need to change the
memory card

메모리 카드를 갈아야 돼요
Me mo ri ka deu reul ga ra ya dwae yo

The flash isn't working

플래쉬가 안돼요
Peul lae swi ga an dwae yo

My computer ran out
of battery

제 컴퓨터 배터리가 다 됐어요
Je com pu ter ba teo ri ga da
dwae seo yo

There is a hardware/
software problem with
the computer

컴퓨터 하드웨어에/소프트웨어에
문제가 있어요
Com pu ter hardware-e/software-e
mun je ga i seo yo

Processing and prints

I'd like to have this film
developed/printed,
please

이 필름 현상/인화 좀 해 주세요
I pil leum hyeon sang/in hwa jom hae
ju se yo

I'd like ... prints from each negative	전부 ... 장씩 뽑아주세요
	Jeon bu ... jang ssik ppo ba ju se yo
glossy/matte	광택지/매트지
	gwang taek ji/mae teu ji
6 x 9	육 구 인치 사이즈
	yuk gu in chi sa i jeu
I'd like to order reprints of these photos	이 사진 좀 더 뽑아 주세요
	I sa jin jom deo ppo ba ju se yo
I'd like to have this photo enlarged	이 사진 좀 확대 해 주세요
	I sa jin jom hwak dae hae ju se yo
How much is processing?	뽑는 데 얼마예요?
	Ppom neun de eol ma ye yo?
How much for printing?	인화하는 데 얼마예요?
	In hwa ha neun de eol ma ye yo?
How much are the reprints?	더 뽑는 데 얼마예요?
	Deo ppom neun de eol ma ye yo?
How much is it for enlargement?	확대하는 데 얼마예요?
	Hwak dae ha neun de eol ma ye yo?
When will they be ready?	언제 될까요?
	Eon je doel kka yo?

10.5 At the hairdresser

Do I have to make an appointment?	예약해야 돼요?
	Ye yak hae ya dwae yo?
Can I come in right now?	지금 당장 가도 돼요?
	Ji geum dang jang ga do dwae yo?
How long will I have to wait?	얼마동안 기다려야 될까요?
	Eol ma dong-an gi da ryeo ya doel kka yo?
I'd like a shampoo/ haircut	샴푸/컷트 좀 해 주세요.
	Syam pu/keo teu jom hae ju se yo.
I'd like a shampoo for oily/dry hair, please	지성/건성 머리용 샴푸 좀 해 주세요
	Ji seong/geon seong meo ri yong syam pu jom hae ju se yo
I'd like an anti-dandruff shampoo	비듬 샴푸 좀 해 주세요
	Bi deum syam pu jom hae ju se yo

I'd like a color-rinse shampoo, please	염색전용 샴푸 좀 해 주세요 Yeom saek jeo nyong syam pu jom hae ju se yo
I'd like a shampoo with conditioner, please	린스겸용 샴푸 좀 해 주세요. Rin seu gyeo myong syam pu jom hae ju se yo
I'd like highlights, please	블리치 좀 넣어주세요 Beul li chi jom neo-eo ju se yo
Do you have a color chart, please?	칼라 견본 있어요? Kal la gyeon bon i sseo yo?
I'd like to keep the same color	지금하고 같은 색으로 좀 해 주세요 Ji geum ha go ga teun sae geu ro jom hae ju se yo
I'd like it darker/lighter	더 어둡게/밝게 좀 해 주세요 Deo eo dup ge/bal kke jom hae ju se yo
I'd like/I don't want hairspray	헤어 스프레이 해 주세요./하지 마세요 He eo seu peu rei hae ju se yo./ha ji ma se yo
gel	젤 jel
lotion	로션 ro syeon
I'd like short bangs	앞머리 짧게 좀 해 주세요 Am meo ri jjal kke jom hae ju se yo
Not too short at the back	뒤는 너무 짧지 않게 해 주세요 Dwi neun neo mu jjal jji anke hae ju se yo
Not too long	너무 길지 않게 해 주세요 Neo mu gil ji an ke hae ju se yo
I'd like it curly/not too curly	곱슬곱슬하게/너무 곱슬곱슬하지 않게 좀 해 주세요 Gop seul gop seul ha ge/neo mu gop seul gop seul ha ji an ke jom hae ju se yo
I'd like a completely different style/cut	완전히 다른 스타일로/컷트로 좀 해 주세요 Wan jeon hi da reun seu ta il lo/ keo teu ro jom hae ju se yo

It needs a little/a lot taken off	약간/많이 좀 쳐 주세요 Yak gan/ma ni jom chyeo ju se yo
I'd like it the same as in this photo	이 사진처럼 좀 해 주세요 I sa jin che reom jom hae ju se yo
as that woman's	저 여자처럼 jeo yeo ja ch reom
Could you turn the drier up/down a bit?	드라이어 좀 올려/내려 주시겠어요? Deu ra i eo jom ol lyeo/nae ryeo ju si ge sseo yo?
I'd like a facial	얼굴 손질 좀 해 주세요 Eol gul son jil jom hae ju se yo
a manicure	손톱 손질 son top son jil
a massage	마사지 ma sa ji
Could you trim my..., please?	제 … 좀 다듬어 주시겠어요? Je … jom da deu meo ju si ge sseo yo?
bangs	앞머리 am meo ri
beard	턱수염 teok su yeom
moustache	콧수염 kot su yeom
I'd like a shave, please	면도 좀 해주세요 Myeon do jom hae ju se yo

어떻게 잘라 드릴까요?	How do you want it cut?
무슨 스타일을 원하세요?	What style did you have in mind?
무슨 칼라를 원하세요?	What color did you want it?
온도가 괜찮으세요?	Is the temperature all right for you?
읽을 거 드릴까요?	Would you like something to read?
마실 거 드릴까요?	Would you like a drink?
이게 원하시던 거예요?	Is this what you had in mind?

11 Tourist Activities

11. Tourist Activities

● **Tourist information and assistance** can easily be obtained from the Tourist Information Center (TIC) of the Korea National Tourism Organization (KNTO) in Seoul. The office is open every day from 9 a.m. to 8 p.m. and its phone number is 82-2-7299-497~499. Tourist information is also available from the Seoul City Tourist Information Centers at major tourist attractions in Seoul, or from the information counters at the three international airports (Incheon, Gimhae, and Jeju), or from major transportation terminals such as railway stations and ferry or bus terminals in major cities. There is also the Korea Travel Phone service offering tourist information and assistance in English. Just call 1330 to get detailed travel information about most areas in the country.

11.1 Places of interest

Where's the Tourist Information, please?	관광 안내소가 어디에 있어요? **Gwan-gwang an nae so ga eo di e i sseo yo?**
Do you have a city map?	시내 지도 있어요? **Si nae ji do i sseo yo?**
Where is the museum?	박물관이 어디에 있어요? **Bang mul gwa ni eo di e i sseo yo?**
Where can I find a church?	교회가 어디에 있어요? **Gyo hoe ga eo di e i sseo yo?**
Could you give me some information about ...?	...에 대해서 안내 좀 해 주시겠어요? **...e dae hae seo an nae jom hae ju si ge sseo yo?**
How much is this?	이거 얼마예요? **I geo eol ma ye yo?**
What are the main places of interest?	관광명소가 어디예요? **Gwan-gwang myeong so ga eo di ye yo?**
What do you recommend?	어디를 추천하시겠어요? **Eo di reul chu cheon ha si ge sseo yo?**
We'll be here for a few hours	여기 두 세 시간 있을 거예요 **Yeo gi du se si gan i sseul geo ye yo**

We'll be here for a day	여기 하루 있을 거예요 Yeo gi ha ru i sseul geo ye yo
We'll be here for a week	여기 일 주일 있을 거예요 Yeo gi il ju il i sseul geo ye yo
We're interested in...	...에 관심이 있어요 ...e gwan si mi i sseo yo
Is there a scenic walk around the city?	시내 근처에 전망이 좋은 산책로 있어요? Si nae geun cheo-e jeon mang-i jo-eun san chaeng no i sseo yo?
How long does it take?	얼마나 걸려요? Eol ma na geol lyeo yo?
Where does it start/end?	어디에서 시작돼요?/끝나요? Eo di e seo si jak dwae yo?/kkeun na yo?
Are there any boat trips?	유람선 투어 있어요? Yu ram seon tu eo i sseo yo?
Where can we board?	어디에서 타요? Eo di e seo ta yo?
Are there any bus tours?	관광버스 투어가 있어요? Gwan.gwang beo seu tu eo ga i sseo yo?
Where do we get on?	어디에서 타요? Eo di e seo ta yo?
Is there a guide who speaks English?	영어 할 줄 아는 가이드 있어요? Yeong-eo hal jul a neun ga i deu I sseo yo?
What trips can we take around the area?	그 지역에 어떤 투어가 있어요? Geu ji yeo ge eo tteon tu eo ga i sseo yo?
Are there any excursions?	야외 투어가 있어요? Ya-oe tu eo ga i sseo yo?
Where do they go?	어디 어디로 가요? Eo di eo di ro ga yo?
We'd like to go to ...	...에 가고 싶어요 ...e jom ga go si peo yo
How long is the excursion?	그 투어는 얼마나 걸려요? Geu tu eo neun eol ma na geol yeo yo?

How long do we stay in ...?	...에 얼마나 오래 있어요? **...eol ma na o rae i sseo yo?**
Are there any guided tours?	가이드 투어가 있어요? **Ga i deu tu eo ga i sseo yo?**
How much free time will we have there?	거기에서 자유시간이 얼마나 있어요? **Geo gi e seo ja yu si ga ni eol ma na i sseo yo?**
We want to have a walk around/to go on foot	걸어서 다니고 싶어요 **Geo reo seo do ra da ni go si peo yo**
Can we hire a guide?	가이드를 고용할 수 있어요? **Ga i deu reul go yong hal su i sseo yo?**
What time does ... open/close?	몇 시에 ...열어요/닫아요? **Myeot si e ...yeo reo yo/da da yo?**
What days is ... open/closed?	무슨 요일에 ...열어요/닫아요? **Mu seun yo i re ...yeo reo yo/da da yo?**
What's the admission price?	입장료가 얼마예요? **Ip jang nyo ga eol ma ye yo?**
Is there a group discount?	단체 할인 돼요? **Dan che ha rin dwae yo?**
Is there a child discount?	어린이 할인 돼요? **Eo ri ni ha rin dwae yo?**
Is there a discount for senior citizens?	경노 할인 돼요? **Gyeong no ha rin dwae yo?**
Can I take (flash) photos here?	(플래쉬) 사진 찍어도 돼요? **(peul lae swi) sa jin jji geo do dwae yo?**
Do you have any postcards of ...?	...엽서 있어요? **...yeop seo i sseo yo?**
Do you have an English ...?	영어 ...있어요? **Yeong.eo ...i sseo yo?**
catalog	카타로그 **ka ta ro geu**
program	프로그램 **peu ro geu raem**
brochure	브로슈어 **beu ro syu eo**

Do you have this week's/month's entertainment guide?	이번 주/달 공연 안내서 있어요? **I beon ju/dal gong-yeon an nae seo i sseo yo?**
What's on tonight?	오늘 저녁에 뭐 해요? **O neul jeo nyeo ge mwo hae yo?**
We want to go to...	...에 가고 싶어요 **...e ga go si peo yo**
What's on at the cinema?	극장에서 뭐 해요? **Geuk jang-e seo mwo hae yo?**
What sort of film is that?	어떤 영화예요? **Eo tteon yeong hwa ye yo?**
suitable for everyone	누구나 볼 수 있는 **nu gu na bol su in neun**
not suitable for people under 18	열여덟 살 이하는 볼 수 없는 **yeol yeo deop sal i ha-neun bol su eop neun**
original version	오리지날 판 **o ri ji nal pan**
subtitled	자막이 나오는 **ja ma gi na o neun**
dubbed	더빙이 된 **deo bing-i doen**
Is it a continuous showing?	연속상영이에요? **Yeon sok sang yeong.l e yo?**
What's on at...?	...에서는 뭐 해요? **...en seo-neuun mwo hae yo?**
the theater	극장 **geuk jang**
the opera	오페라 극장 **o pe ra geuk jang**
Where can I find a good night club around here?	이 근처에서 좋은 나이트 클럽이 어디에 있어요? **i geun cheo-e seo jo-eun na i teu keul leo pi eo di e i sseo yo?**

What's happening in the concert hall?	콘서트 홀에서는 뭐 해요? Kon seo teu ho re seo neun mwo hae yo?
Is it members only?	회원 전용이에요? Hoe won jeo nyong-i e yo?
Is it evening wear only?	야회복을 꼭 입어야 돼요? Ya hoe bo geul kkok i beo ya dwae yo?
Should I/we dress up?	정장을 입어야 돼요? Jeong jang eul i beo ya dwae yo?
What time does the show start?	몇 시에 공연이 시작돼요? Myeot si e gong yeo ni si jak dwae yo?
When's the next soccer match?	다음 축구경기가 언제 있어요? Da-eum chu gu gyeong ga eon je i sseo yo?
I'd like an escort for tonight	오늘 저녁에 파트너가 필요해요 O neul jeo nyeo ge pa teu neo ga pi ryo hae yo

11.3 Booking tickets

Could you reserve some tickets for us?	티켓을 몇 장 예약해 주시겠어요? Ti ke teul myeot jang ye yak hae ju si ge sseo yo?
We'd like to book... seats/a table for...	좌석 ...개/...인용 테이블 하나를 예약하고 싶어요. Jwa seok ...gae/...i nyong te i beul ha nar eul ye yak ha go si peo yo
...seats in the orchestra in the main section	오케스트라석 ...장 o ke seu teu ra seok ...jang
a box for...	...인용 박스석 하나 ...i nyong bak seu seok ha na
...seats in the middle/a table in the middle	중간 좌석 ...장/중간 테이블 하나 jung gan jwa seok ...jang/jung gan te i beul ha na
...back row seats/a table at the back	뒷줄 좌석 ...징/뒤쪽 데이블 하나 dwit jul jwa seok ...jang/dwi jjok te i beul ha na

...front row seats/a table for...at the front	앞줄 좌석 ...장/...인용 앞쪽 테이블 하나 **ap jul jwa seok ...jang/...i nyong ap jjok te i beul ha na**
Could I reserve...seats for the...o'clock performance?	...시 공연 좌석 ...장 예약해 주시겠어요? **...si gong-yeon jwa seok ...jang ye yak hae ju si ge sseo yo?**
Are there any seats left for tonight?	오늘 저녁 좌석 남은 거 있어요? **O neul jeo nyeok jwa seok na meun geo i sseo yo?**
How much is a ticket?	티켓 한 장에 얼마예요? **Ti ket han jang.e eol ma ye yo?**
When can I pick up the tickets?	인제 티켓 찾으러 갈까요? **Eon je ti ket cha jeu reo gal kka yo?**
I've got a reservation	예약했어요 **Ye yak hae sseo yo**

어느 공연을 예약하시고 싶으세요?	Which performance do you want to reserve for?
어디에 앉으시고 싶으세요?	Where would you like to sit?
전부 매진입니다	Everything's sold out
입석만 있습니다	It's standing room only
이층석민 남았습니다	We've only got circle seats left
삼층석반 남았습니다	We've only got upper circle (way upstairs) seats left
오케스트라석만 남았습니다	We've only got orchestra seats left
앞줄 좌석만 남았습니다	We've only got front row seats left
뒷줄 좌석만 남았습니다	We've only got seats left at the back
좌석 몇 개가 필요하세요?	How many seats would you like?
...시 이전에 티켓을 찾아 가셔야 합니다	You'll have to pick up the tickets before...o'clock
티켓, 부탁합니다	Tickets, please
여기가 손님 좌석입니다	This is your seat
좌석을 잘못 앉으셨어요	You are in the wrong seat

12

Sports
Activities

12. Sports Activities

● **Many beaches, lakes and rivers** including the Han River in Seoul offer a wide range of summer sports such as water skiing, canoeing, scuba diving, wind surfing and rafting. There are also several world-class ski resorts that are open from mid December until early March. During the season, major travel agencies operate bus trips between Seoul and the resorts. The most popular spectator sports are baseball and soccer.

12.1 Sporting questions

Where can we ... around here?	이 근처 어디에서 ...(으)ㄹ 수 있어요? I geun cheo eo di e seo -(eu)l su i sseo yo?
Can we hire a ...?	...빌릴 수 있어요? ...bil lil su i sseo yo?
Can we take ... lessons?	...강습 받을 수 있어요? ...gang seup ba deul su i sseo yo?
How much is that per hour/per day?	시간에/하루에 얼마예요? Si ga ne/ha ru e eol ma ye yo?
How much is each one?	각 각 얼마예요? Gak gak eol ma ye yo?
Do you need a permit for that?	허가를 받아야 돼요? Heo ga reul ba da ya dwae yo?
Where can I get the permit?	어디에서 허가를 받을 수 있어요? Eo di e seo heo ga reul ba deul su i sseo yo?

12.2 By the waterfront

Is it far (to walk) to the sea?	바다까지 (걷기에) 멀어요? Ba da kka ji (geot gi e) meo reo yo?
Is there a...around here?	이 근처에 ...있어요? I geun cheo-e ...i sseo yo?

a swimming pool	수영장 su yeong jang
a sandy beach	모래 사장 mo rae sa jang
mooring place	선착장 seon chak jang
Are there any sunken rocks here?	여기 암초가 있어요? Yeo gi am cho ga i sseo yo?
When is high/low tide?	썰물이/밀물이 언제예요? Sseol mu ri/mil mu ri eon je ye yo?
What's the water temperature?	수온은 어떻게 돼요? Su o neun eo tteo ke dwae yo?
Is it (very) deep here?	여기 (아주) 깊어요? Yeo gi (aju) gi peo yo?
Is it safe (for children) to swim here?	여기 (어린이가) 수영하기가 안전해요? Yeo gi (eo rin ga) su yeong ha gi ga an jeon hae yo?
Are there any currents?	물살이 강한 곳이 있어요? Mul sa ri gang-han go si i sseo yo?
Are there any rapids/ waterfalls along this river?	이 강에 급류가/폭포가 있어요? I gang-e geum nyu ga/pok po ga i sseo yo?
What does that flag/ buoy mean?	저 깃발이/부표가 무슨 뜻이에요? Jeo git ba ri/bu pyo ga mu seun tteu si e yo?
Is there a lifeguard on duty?	인명 구조원이 있어요? In myeong gu jo wo ni i sseo yo?
Are dogs allowed here?	여기 개를 데리고 와도 돼요? Yeo gi gae reul de ri go wa do dwae yo?
Is camping on the beach allowed?	바닷가에서 캠핑해도 돼요? Ba dat ga-e seo kaem ping.hae do dwae yo?
Can we light a fire?	불을 피워도 돼요? Bu reul pi wo do dwae yo?

낚시터	서핑금지	수영금지
Fishing waters	No surfing	No swimming

면허소지자자에 한함	위험	낚시금지
Permits only	Danger	No fishing

In the snow

Can I take ski lessons here?	여기에서 스키강습 받을 수 있어요? Ye gi e seo seu ki gang seup ba deul su i sseo yo?
for beginners/ intermediates/advanced	초급/중급/고급 cho geup/jung geup/go geup
How large are the groups?	반이 얼마나 커요? Ba ni eol ma na keo yo?
What languages are the classes in?	강습에서 어떤 언어를 써요? Gang seu be seo eo tteon eo neo reul sseo yo?
I'd like a lift pass, please	리프트 패스 하나 주세요 Ri peu teu pae seu ha na ju se yo
Where are the beginner's slopes?	초급 코스는 어디에 있어요? Cho geup ko seu neun eo di e i sseo yo?
Are there any cross-country ski runs around here?	크로스 칸츄리 코스가 있어요? Reu ro seu kan chyu ri ko seu ga i sseo yo?
Have the cross-country runs been marked?	크로스 카츄리 코스에 표시가 있어요? Keu ro seu kan chyu ri ko seu e pyo si ga i sseo yo?
Are the ... open?	...열있어요? ...yeo reot seo yo?
the ski lifts	스키 리프트 seu ki ri peu teu
the chair lifts	리프트 ri peu teu
the runs	코스 ko seu
the cross-country runs	크로스 칸츄리 코스 keu ro seu kan chyu ri ko seu

13 Health Matters

13. Health Matters

● **You can see** any specialist or doctor without having a GP's referral. Most doctors in hospitals in Korea speak some basic English. However, if you are in Seoul, it is recommended that you see the doctors in the International Clinics of general hospitals such as the Severance Hospital, Asan Medical Centre, or Samsung Medical Centre. You can buy medication for common illnesses over the counter at pharmacists without a doctor's prescription.

13.1 Calling a doctor

Could you call a doctor quickly, please?	의사 좀 빨리 불러 주시겠어요? Ui sa jom ppal li bul leo ju si ge sseo yo?
When is the doctor in?	진료시간이 어떻게 돼요? Jil lyo si ga ni eo tteo ke dwae yo?
When can the doctor come?	언제 의사가 올 수 있어요? Eon je ui sa ga ol su i sseo yo?
Could I make an appointment to see the doctor?	진료예약을 할 수 있을까요? Jil lyo ye ya geul hal su i sseul kka yo?
I've got an appointment to see the doctor at ...o'clock	...시에 진료예약을 했어요 ...si e jil lyo ye ya geul hae sseo yo
Which doctor/pharmacy is on night/weekend duty?	어느 의사가/약국이 밤에/수말에 일해요? Eo neu ui sa ga/yak gu gi ba me/ju ma re il hae yo?

13.2 What's wrong?

I don't feel well	몸이 안 좋아요 Mo mi an jo a yo
I'm dizzy	어지러워요 Eo ji reo wo yo

I'm sick.	아파요 A pa yo
I feel nauseous	메스꺼워요 Me s kkeo wo yo
I've got a cold	감기에 걸렸어요 Gam gi e geol lyeo sseo yo
It hurts here	여기가 아파요 Yeo gi ga a pa yo
I vomited	토했어요 To hae sseo yo
I've got ...	...이/가 있어요 ...i/ga i sseo yo
I'm running a temperature of ...degrees	체온이 ...도나 돼요. Ch o ni ...do na dwae yo
I've been stung by ...	...에 쏘였어요 ...e sso yeo sseo yo
a wasp	벌 beol
an insect	벌레 beol le
a jellyfish	해파리 hae pa ri
I've been bitten by...	...에 물렸어요 ...e mul lyeo sseo yo
a dog	개 gae
a snake	뱀 baem
an animal	동물 dong mul
I've cut myself	상처를 냈어요 Sang cheo reul nae sseo yo
I've burned myself	화상을 입었어요 Hwa sang-eul i beo sseo yo
I've grazed myself	찰과상을 입었어요 Chal gwa sang-eul i beo sseo yo

I've had a fall	넘어졌어요
	Neo meo jyeo sseo yo
I've sprained my ankle	발목을 삐었어요
	Bal mo geul ppi eo sseo yo

13.3 The consultation

어떤 문제인 것 같아요?	What seems to be the problem?
이런 증세가 얼마나	How long have you had
오래됐어요?	these complaints?
전에 이런 문제가 있었어요?	Have you had this trouble before?
열이 있어요? 얼마나	Do you have a temperature?
높아요?	What is it?
옷을 벗으세요	Get undressed, please
허리까지 벗으세요	Strip to the waist, please
저기에서 벗으시면 돼요	You can undress there
왼쪽/오른쪽 소매를 걷어	Roll up your left/right sleeve,
올려 주세요	please
여기에 누우세요	Lie down here, please
이렇게 하면 아파요?	Does this hurt?
숨을 깊이 쉬세요	Breathe deeply
입을 벌리세요	Open your mouth

Patient's medical history

I'm a diabetic	당뇨병이 있어요
	Dan nyo byeong-i i sseo yo
I have a heart condition	심장질환이 있어요
	Sim jang jil hwa ni i sseo yo
I'm asthmatic	천식이 있어요
	Cjeon si gi i sseo yo
I'm allergic to ...	...에 알레르기가 있어요
	...al le reu gi ga i sseo yo
I'm ...months pregnant	임신 ...개월이에요
	Im sin ...gae wo ri e yo

I'm on a diet	지금 식이요법을 하고 있어요 Ji geum si gi yo ppeo beul ha go i sseo yo
I'm on medication	지금 약을 먹고 있어요 Ji geum ya geul meok go i sseo yo
I've had a heart attack once before	전에 한번 심장마비를 한 적이 있어요 Jeo ne han beon sim jang ma bi ga on jeo gi i sseo yo
I've had a(n) ...operation	...수술을 한 적이 있어요 ...su su reul han jeo gi i sseo yo
I've been ill recently	최근에 아팠어요 Choe geu ne a pa sseo yo
I've got a stomach ulcer	위궤양이 있어요 Wi gwe yang-i i sseo yo
I've got my period	생리 중이에요 Saeng-ni jung.i e yo

알레르기가 있어요?	Do you have any allergies?
지금 약을 복용 중이신가요?	Are you on any medication?
지금 식이요법 중 이신가요?	Are you on a diet?
임신 중이신가요?	Are you pregnant?
파상풍 주사를 맞으신 적이 있나요?	Have you had a tetanus injection?

The diagnosis

심각한 건 아니에요	It's nothing serious
...이/가 부러졌네요	Your ...is broken
...삐었군요.	You've got a sprained ...
...이/가 찢어졌군요	You've got a torn ...
염증이 있군요	You've got some inflammation
맹장염이군요	You've got appendicitis

기관지염이군요	You've got bronchitis
성병이군요	You've got a venereal disease
독감이군요	You've got the flu
심장마비이군요	You've had a heart attack
(바이러스성/박테리아성) 염증이에요	You've got a (viral/ bacterial) infection
폐렴이에요	You've got pneumonia
위염/위궤양이에요	You've got gastritis/an ulcer
근육이 늘어났군요	You've pulled a muscle
질염이군요	You've got a vaginal infection
식중독이에요	You've got food poisoning
일사병이에요	You've got sunstroke
...에 알레르기가 있군요	You're allergic to ...
임신이군요	You're pregnant
피/소변/대변 검사를 해야겠어요	I'd like to have your blood/ urine/stools tested
봉합 수술이 필요해요	It needs stitches
전문의한테 보내드리겠어요	I'm referring you to a specialist
엑스레이를 찍어야겠어요	You'll need some x-rays taken
대기실에서 좀 기다려 주시겠어요?	Could you wait in the waiting room, please?
수술을 해야겠어요	You'll need an operation

Is it contagious?	이거 전염돼요? I geo jeo nyeom dwae yo?
How long do I have to stay ...?	얼마나 오래 ...있어야 돼요? Eol ma na o rae ...i sseo ya dwae yo?
in bed	누워 nu wo
in the hospital	병원에 byeong-wo ne
Do I have to go on a special diet?	식이요법을 해야 돼요? Si gi yo beo beul hae ya dwae yo?
Am I allowed to travel?	여행을 해도 돼요? Yeo haeng-eul hae do dwae yo?
Can I make another appointment?	다음 예약 할 수 있어요? Da eum ye ya geul hal su i sseo yo?

When do I have to come back?	언제 다시 와야 돼요? Eon je da si wa ya dwae yo?
I'll come back tomorrow	내일 다시 오겠어요 Nae il da si o ge sseo yo
How do I take this medicine?	이 약 어떻게 먹어요? I yak eo tteo ke meo geo yo?

| 내일/...일 후에 다시 오세요 | Come back tomorrow/in
...days' time |

13.4 Medications and prescriptions

How many pills/drops/ spoonfuls/tablets each time?	한 번에 몇 알/방울/스푼/알씩이에요? Han beo ne myeot al/bang-ul/seu pun/ al ssi gi e yo?
How many times a day?	하루에 몇 번씩이요? Ha ru e myeot beon ssi gi yo?
I've forgotten my medication	약 먹는 것을 잊어버렸어요 Yak meong neun geo seul i jeo beo ryeo sseo yo
Could you write a prescription for me, please?	처방전 좀 써 주시겠어요? Cheo bang jeon jom sseo ju si ge sseo yo?

항생제/감기 물약/진정제/ 진통제 처방 해드릴께요	I'm prescribing antibiotics/a cough mixture/a tranquilizer/pain killers
푹 쉬세요	Have lots of rest
집에 계세요	Stay indoors
누워 계세요	Stay in bed

| 캡슐 | 물에 녹이세요 | (통째로) 삼키세요 |
| capsules | dissolve in water | swallow (whole) |

알약	고루 바르세요	외용
pills/tablets	rub on	External use only
점적약	...일 동안	이 약은 운전에 장애를
drops	for ...days	가져옵니다
		This medication impairs
		your driving
주사	식전에	처방전의 약을 끝까지
injections	before meals	드세요
연고	매 ...시간마다	Finish the prescription
ointment	every ...hours	
드세요	하루에 ...번씩	한 숟갈/ 한 찻숟갈
take	...times a day	spoonful/teaspoonful

13.5 At the dentist

Do you know a good dentist?	잘 하는 지과 의사 아세요?
	Jal ha neun chi kkwa ui sa a se yo?
Could you make a dental appointment for me?	치과에 예약 좀 해 주시겠어요?
	Chi kkwa-e ye yak jom hae ju si ge sseo yo?
It's urgent	급해요
	Geu pae yo
Can I come in today, please?	오늘 가도 돼요?
	O neul ga do dwae yo?
I have a (terrible) toothache	이가 (심하게) 아파요
	I ga (sim ha ge) a pa yo
Could you prescribe/give me a painkiller?	진통제 좀 처방해 주시겠어요?
	Ji tong je jom cheo bang hae ju si ge sseo yo?
I've got a broken tooth	이가 부러졌어요
	I ga bu reo jyeo sseo yo
My filling's come out	이 떼운 게 빠졌어요
	I ttae un ge ppa jyeo sseo yo
I've got a broken crown	이 씌운 게 망가졌어요
	I sswi un ge mang-ga jyeo sseo yo

I'd like/I don't want a local anaesthetic

국부 마취를 해 주세요/하지 마세요
Guk bu ma chwi reul hae ju se yo/ha ji ma se yo

Could you do a temporary repair?

임시처방을 좀 해 주시겠어요?
Im si cheo bang-eul jom hae ju si ge sseo yo?

I don't want this tooth pulled

이 이를 빼고 싶지 않아요
I i reul ppae go sip ji a na yo

My denture is broken

틀니가 망가졌어요
Teul li ga mang-ga jyeo sseo yo

Can you fix it?

고칠 수 있어요?
Go chil su i sseo yo?

어느 이가 아프세요?	Which tooth hurts?
고름이 생겼어요	You've got an abscess
근관치료를 해야겠어요	I'll have to do a root canal
국부 마취를 해야겠어요	I'm giving you a local anaesthetic
이 이를 뽑아야/떼워야/갈아야 되겠어요	I'll have to pull/fill/file this tooth
드릴을 해야겠어요	I'll have to drill it
입을 크게 벌리세요	Open wide, please
입을 다무세요	Close your mouth, please
입을 헹구세요	Rinse, please
아직도 아프세요?	Does it hurt still?

14 Emergencies

14. Emergencies

● **In an emergency**, call 112 for the police and 119 for the fire or ambulance service. Many police boxes are located on the major streets of most cities. Alternatively, you can call the International SOS Korea (Tel: 82 (2) 3140 1700) for 24-hour emergency service assistance in English. For lost property, contact the Lost and Found Center of the Seoul Metropolitan Police Agency (Tel: 82-1566-0112).

14.1 Asking for help

Help!	도와 주세요! **Do wa ju se yo!**
Fire!	불이 났어요! **Bu ri na sseo yo!**
Police!	경찰요! **Gyeong cha ryo!**
Quick/Hurry!	빨리요! **Ppal li yo!**
Danger!	위험해요! **Wi heom hae yo!**
Watch out!	조심하세요! **Jo sim ha se yo!**
Stop!	멈추세요! **Meom ch se yo!**
Be careful!/Go easy!	조심하세요! **Jo sim ha se yo!**
Get your hands off me!	손 치워요! **Son chi wo yo!**
Stop thief!	도둑이야! **Do du gi ya!**
Could you help me, please?	저 좀 도와 주시겠어요? **Jeo jom do wa ju si ge sseo yo?**

Where's the police emergency exit/ fire escape?	경찰서/비상구/비상구가 어디에 있어요? Gyeong chal seo/bi sang-gu/bi sang-gu ga eo di e i sseo yo?
Where's the nearest fire extinguisher?	소화기가 어디에 있어요? So hwa gi ga eo di e i sseo yo?
Call the fire department!	소방서에 연락하세요! So bang seo-e yeol lak ha se yo!
Call the police!	경찰에 연락하세요! Gyeong cha le yeol lak ha se yo!
Call an ambulance!	앰뷸런스를 부르세요! Am byul leon seu reul bu reu se yo!
Where's the nearest phone?	전화가 어디에 있어요? Jen hwa ga eo di e i sseo yo?
Could I use your phone?	전화 좀 써도 돼요? Jeon hwa jom sseo do dwae yo?
What's the emergency number?	응급 전화가 몇 번이에요? Eung geup jeon hwa ga myeot neo ni e yo?
What's the number for the police?	경찰 전화가 몇 번이에요? Gyeong chal jeon hwa ga myeot neo ni e yo?
I've lost my wallet/purse	지갑을 잃어버렸어요 Ji ga beul i reo beo ryeo sseo yo

Lost items

I lost my ...here yesterday	어제 여기서 ...을/를 잃어버렸어요 Eo ja yeo gi seo ...eul/reul i reo beo ryeo sseo yo
I left my ...here	여기에 ...을/를 두었어요 Yeo gi e ...eul/reul du eo sseo yo
Did you find my...?	제 ... 찾았어요? Je ... cha ja sseo yo?
It was right here	바로 여기에 있었어요 Ba ro yeo gi e i sseo sseo yo
It's very valuable	아주 소중한 거예요 A ju so jung-han geo ye yo

| Where's the lost and found office? | 분실물센터가 어디에 있어요?
Bun sil mul sen teo ga eo di e i sseo yo? |

14.3 Accidents

There's been an accident	사고가 났어요 Sa go ga na sseo yo
Someone's fallen into the water	누가 물에 빠졌어요 Nu ga mu re ppa jyeo sseo yo
There's a fire	불이 났어요 Bu ri na sseo yo
Is anyone hurt?	다친 사람 있어요? Da chin sa ram i sseo yo?
Nobody has been injured	아무도 안 다쳤어요 A mu do an da chyeo sseo yo
Someone has been injured	누가 다쳤어요 Nu ga da chyeo sseo yo
Someone's still trapped inside the car/train	누가 아직도 차/기차 안에 갇혀 있어요 Nu ga a jik do cha/gi cha a ne gat chyeo i sseo yo
It's not too bad	아주 나쁘진 않아요 A ju na ppeu jin a na yo
Don't worry	걱정하지 마세요 Geok jeong ha ji ma se yo
Leave everything the way it is, please	있는 그대로 두세요 In neun geu dae ro du se yo
I want to talk to the police first	먼저 경찰에 신고해야겠어요 Meon jeo gyeong cha re sin.go hae ya ge sseo yo
I want to take a photo first	먼저 사진을 찍어야겠어요 Meon jeo sa ji neul jji geo ya ge sseo yo
Here's my name and address	여기 제 이름과 주소가 있어요 Yeo gi je i reum gwa ju so ga i sseo yo
May I have your name and address?	성함과 주소 좀 주시겠어요? Seong-ham gwa ju so jom ju si ge sseo yo?

Could I see your identity card/your insurance papers?	신분증/보험증 좀 보여 주시겠어요? **Sin bun jjeung/bo heom jjeung jom bo yeo ju si ge sseo yo?**
Would you act as a witness?	증인이 좀 돼 주시겠어요? **Jeung-i ni jom dwae ju si ge sseo yo?**
I need this information for insurance purposes	보험 청구에 이 내용이 필요해요 **Bo heom cheong-gu e i nae young.i pi ryo hae yo**
Are you insured?	보험 들었어요? **Bo heom deu reo sseo yo?**
Third party or all inclusive?	삼자 대물 보험 아니면 종합 보험이에요? **Sam ja dae mul bo heom a ni myeon jong hap bo heo mi e yo?**
Could you sign here, please?	여기 사인 좀 해 주시겠어요? **Yeo gi sa in jom hae ju si ge sseo yo?**

14.4 Theft

I've been robbed	도둑맞았어요 **Do duk ma ja sseo yo**
My... has been stolen	...을/를 도둑맞았어요 **...eul/reul do duk ma ja sseo yo**
My car's been broken into	제 차에 도둑이 들었어요 **Je cha-e do du gi deu reo sseo yo**

14.5 Missing person

I've lost my child/ grandmother	우리 애/할머니가 없어졌어요 **Uri ae/hal meo ni ga eop seo jyeo sseo yo**
Could you help me find him/her?	좀 찾아주시겠어요? **Jom cha ja ju si ge sseo yo?**
Have you seen a small child?	어린 아이를 못 보셨나요? **Eo rin a i reul mot bo syeoss na yo?**

Emergencies

14

He's/She's ...years old	나이는 ...살이에요
	Na i neun ...sa ri e yo
He/She's got ...hair	...머리예요
	...meo ri ye yo
short/long	짧은/긴
	jjal beun/gin
blond/red/brown/ black/grey	금발/빨간색/갈색/검은색/회색
	geum bal/ppal gan saek/gal saek/ geo meun saek/hoe saek
curly/straight/frizzy	웨이브가 있는/일자/곱슬곱슬한
	we i beu ga in neun/il ja/ gop seul gop seul han
in a ponytail	뒤로 묶은
	dwi ro mu kkeon
in braids	땋은
	tta eun
in a bun	뒤로 올린
	dwi ro ol lin
He's/She's got blue/ brown/green eyes	눈은 파란색/갈색/푸른색 눈이에요
	Nu neun pa ran saek/gal sek/ pu reun saek nu ni e yo
He's/She's wearing swimming trunks/ swimsuit	반바지 수영복을 입고 있어요
	Ban ba ji su yeong bo geul ip go i sseo yo
He's/She's wearing hiking boots	등산화를 신고 있어요
	Deung san hwa reul sin kko i sseo yo
with/without glasses	안경을 끼고/안 끼고
	An gyeong-eul kki go/an kki go
carrying/not carrying a bag	가방을 들고/안 들고
	Ga bang-eul deul go/an deul go
He/She is tall/short	키가 커요/작아요
	Ki ga keo yo/ja ga yo
This is a photo of him/her	이게 그 애 사진이에요
	I ge geu ae sa ji ni e yo
He/she must be lost	틀림없이 길을 잃었어요
	Teul li meop si gi reul i reo sseo yo

14.6 The police

An arrest

면허증 좀 보여 주세요	Your driver's license, please
속도위반입니다	You were speeding
여기 주차하시면 안 됩니다	You're not allowed to park here
주차비를 안 내셨습니다	You haven't put money in the parking meter
라이트가 안 들어옵니다	Your lights aren't working
... 원 벌금입니다	That's a ... won fine
지금 내시겠습니까?	Do you want to pay now?
지금 내셔야 합니다	You'll have to pay now

I don't speak Korean
한국말 못 합니다
Hang gung mal mot ham ni da

I didn't see the sign
표지판을 못 봤어요
Pyo ji pa neul mot bwa sseo yo

I don't understand what it says
무슨 말인지 모르겠어요
Mu seun ma rin ji mo reu geo sseo yo

I was only doing ... kilometers an hour
시속 ... 키로였는데요
Dan ji ... ki ro yeon neun de yo

I'll have my car checked
차 정비를 맡기겠어요
Cha jeong ni reul mat gi geo sseo yo

I was blinded by oncoming lights
맞은편 차량 불빛 때문에 볼 수가 없었어요
Ma jeun pyeon cha ryang bul bit-ttae mu ne bol su ga eop sseo sseo yo

어디서 일어났습니까?	Where did it happen?
뭐가 없어졌습니까?	What's missing?
뭘 가져갔습니까?	What's been taken?
신분증 좀 보여 주시겠습니까?	Could I see your identity card/ some identification?

그게 몇 시였습니까?   What time did it happen?
증인이 있습니까?   Are there any witnesses?
여기 서명하세요   Sign here, please
통역이 필요하십니까?   Do you want an interpreter?

At the police station

I want to report a
collision/missing
person/rape

추돌 사고를/실종사건을/강간사건을
신고하 고싶어요
**Chung dol sa go reul/sil jjong
sa kkeu neul/gang-gan sa kkeo neul
sin.go ha go si peo yo**

Could you make a
statement, please?

진술서를 좀 써 주시겠어요?
**Jin sul seo reul jom sseo
ju si ge sseo yo?**

Could I have a copy for
the insurance?

보험용으로 사본 한 장 좀 주시겠어요?
**Bo heom yong-eu ro sa bon han jang
jom ju si ge sseo yo?**

I've lost everything

다 잃어버렸어요
Da i reo beo ryeo sseo yo

I've no money left

돈이 하나도 없어요
Do ni ha na do eop seo yo

Could you lend me a
little money?

돈을 조금 빌려 주시겠어요?
**Do neul jo geum bil lyeo
ju si ge sseo yo?**

I'd like an interpreter

통역이 필요해요
Tong yeo gi pi ryo hae yo

I'm innocent

저는 죄가 없어요
Je neun joe ga eop seo yo

I don't know anything
about it

그에 대해서 아무것도 모릅니다
**Geu e dae hae seo a mu geot do
mo reum ni da**

I want to speak to
someone from
the ... embassy

... 대사관 직원과 얘기하고 싶어요 ...
**Dae sa gwan ji gwon-gwa yae gi ha go
si peo yo**

I want a lawyer who
speaks English

영어를 하는 변호사를 불러주세요
**Yeong-eo reul ha neun byeon ho sa reul
bul leo ju se yo**

15 English-Korean Word List

15. English-Korean Word List

● **This word list** is meant to supplement the previous chapters. Some of the words not on this list can be found elsewhere in this book. Food items can be found in Section 4.7, the parts of the car on pages 66-67, the parts of a motorcycle/bicycle on pages 72-73 and camping/backpacking equipment on pages 96-97.

A

about, approximately	...정도	...jeong do
about, regarding	...에 대해	...e dae hae
above, upstairs	...위에	...wi e
abroad	해외에(서)	hae-oe-e(seo)
accident	사고	sa go
adaptor	어댑터	eo daep teo
address	주소	ju so
admission	입장	ip jang
admission price	입장료	ip jang nyo
adult	어른	eo reun
advice	충고	chung go
aeroplane	비행기	bi haeng gi
after	(place) 뒤에,	...dwi e
	(time) 후에	...hu e
afternoon	오후	o hu
aftershave	애프터 쉐이브	ae peu teo swe i beu
again	다시	da si
age	나이	na i
AIDS	에이즈	e i jeu
air conditioning	냉난방	naeng nan bang
air mattress	공기 매트리스	gong gi mae teu ri seu
airmail	항공 우편	hang gong u pyeon
airplane	비행기	bi haeng gi
airport	공항	gong hang
alarm (emergency)	경보	gyeong bo
alarm clock	알람 시계	al lam si gye
alcohol, liquor	술	sul
all day	종일	jong-il
all the time	항상	hang sang
allergy	알레르기	al le reu gi
alone	혼자 있다, 혼자(서)	hon ja it da, hon ja (seo)
altogether, in total	모두	mo du
always	항상	hang sang
ambassador	대사	dae sa
ambulance	앰뷸런스	aem byul leon seu
America	미국	mi guk
American	미국 사람	mi guk sa ram
amount	양, 금액	yang, geu maek
amusement park	놀이 공원	no ri gong-won
anaesthetic (general)	전신 마취	jeon sin ma chwi

anaesthetic (local)	국부 마취	guk bu ma chwi
angry	화나다, 화난	hwa na da, hwa nan
animal	동물	dong mul
ankle	발목	bal mok
answer the phone, to	전화 받다	jeon hwa bat da
answer, respond (written), to	답장하다	dap jang ha da
answer, respond, to	대답하다	dae dap ha da
answer, response (spoken)	대답	dae dap
answer, response (written)	답장	dap jang
answering machine	자동 응답기	ja dong eung dap gi
ant	개미	gae mi
antibiotics	항생제	hang saeng je
antifreeze	부동액	bu dong-aek
antiques	골동품	gol ttong pum
antiseptic	소독약	so dong-yak
anus	항문	hang mun
anybody, anyone	누구든지	nu gu deun ji
anything	무엇이든지	mu eo si deun ji
anywhere	어디든지	eo di deun ji
apartment	아파트	a pa teu
apologise, to	사과하다	sa gwa ha da
apple	사과	sa gwa
apple juice	사과주스	sa gwa ju seu
apply (for permission), to	신청하다	sin cheong ha da
appointment	약속, 임명	yak sok, im myeong
April	사월	sa wol
architecture	건축	geon chuk
area	지역	ji yeok
area code	지역 번호	ji yeok beon ho
arm	팔	pal
arrange, to	준비하다	jun bi ha da
arrival	도착	do chak
arrive, to	도착하다	do chak ha da
arrow	화살	hwa sal
art	예술	ye sul
art gallery	미술관	mi sul gwan
artery	동맥	dong maek
article (in newspaper)	기사	gi sa
ashtray	재떨이	jae tteo ri
ask, to	물어보다	mu reo bo da
ask for, request, to	부탁하다	bu tak ha da
aspirin	아스피린	a seu pi rin
assault	폭행	pok haeng
assorted	종합한	jong hap han
at home	집에	ji be
at night	밤에	ba me
at the back	뒤에	dwi e
at the front	앞에	a pe
at the latest	늦어도	neu jeo do
attractive	매력적이다/-적인	mae ryeok jeo gi da, mae ryeok jeo gin
aubergine, eggplant	가지	ga ji
August	팔월	pa rwol
Australia	호주	ho ju
Australian	호주 사람	ho ju sa ram
automatic	자동	ja dong
autumn	가을	ga-eul

awake	깨어 있는	kkae-eo i neun
awning	차양	cha yang

B

baby	아기	a gi
baby food	이유식	i yu sik
babysitter	보모	bo mo
back (part of body)	등	deung
back, rear	뒤	dwi
backpack	배낭	bae nang
backpacker	배낭 여행자	bae nang yeo haeng ja
backward	뒤로	dwi ro
bad (rotting)	상하다, 상한	sang ha da, sang han
bad (terrible)	나쁘다, 나쁜	na ppeu da, na ppeun
bag	가방	ga bang
bakery	빵집	ppang jjip
balcony	발코니	bal ko ni
ball	공	gong
ball point pen	볼펜	bol pen
banana	바나나	ba na na
bandage	붕대	bung dae
bandaids	일회용 반창고	il hoe yong ban chang go
bangs, fringe	앞머리	am meo ri
bank (finance)	은행	eun haeng
bank (river)	둑	duk
bar (café)	카페	ka pe
barbecue	바베큐	ba be kyu
bargain, to	흥정하다	heung jeong ha da
baseball	야구	ya gu
basketball	농구	nong gu
bath	목욕	mo gyok
bath towel	목욕 타월	mo gyok ta wol
bath mat	목욕탕 매트	mo gyok tang mae teu
bathrobe	목욕 가운	mo gyok ga un
bathroom	화장실, 목욕실	hwa jang sil, mo gyok sil
battery	배터리, 건전지	bae teo ri/battery, geon jeon ji
beach	바닷가	ba dat ga
beans	콩	kong
beautiful (of people)	예쁘다, 예쁜	ye ppeu da, ye ppeun
beautiful (of places)	아름답다/-다운	a reum dap da, a reum da un
beautiful (of things)	멋지다, 멋진	meot ji da, meot jin
because	-기 때문에	-gi ttae mu ne
become, to	되다	doe da
bed	침대	chim dae
bedding, bedclothes	침구	chim gu
bee	벌	beol
beef	쇠고기	soe go gi
beer	맥주	maek ju
before (in front of)	앞에	a pe
before (in time)	전에	jeo ne
begin, to	시작하다	si jak ha da
behind	뒤에	dwi e
below, downstairs	아래에	a rea-e
belt	벨트	bel teu
berth	침대	chim dae

beside	옆에	yeo pe
better, get (improve), to	좋아지다	jo a ji da
between	…사이에	…sa i e
bicycle	자전거	ja jeon-geo
big	크다, 큰	keu da, keun
bikini	비키니	bi ki ni
bill	계산서	gye san seo
billiards	당구	dang gu
birthday	생일	saeng-il
biscuit	비스켓, 과자	bi seu ket, gwa ja
bite, to	물다	mul da
bitter	쓰다, 쓴	sseu da, sseun
black	까맣다, 까만	kka ma ta, kka man
black and white	흑백	heuk baek
black eye	멍든 눈	meong deun nun
bland (taste)	무미하다/-한	mu mi ha da/-han
blanket	담요	dam nyo
bleach, to	탈색하다	tal saek ha da
bleed, to	피를 흘리다	pi reul heul li da
blind (can't see)	눈이 멀다, 눈먼	nu ni meol da, nun meon
blind (on window)	블라인드	beul la in deu
blister	물집	mul jjip
blog	블로그	beul lo geu/blog
blond	금발	geum bal
blood	피	pi
blood pressure	혈압	hyeo rap
bloody nose, to have	코피가 나다	ko pi ga na da
blouse	블라우스	beul la u seu
blue	파랗다, 파란	pa ra ta, pa ran
boat	배	bae
body	몸	mom
boiled	끓인, 삶은	kkeu rin, sal meun
bone	뼈	ppyeo
book	책	chaek
booked, reserved	예약되다, 예약된	ye yak doe da, ye yak doen
booking office	에매소	ye mae so
bookshop	서전	seo jeom
border, edge	기장자리	ga jang ja ri
bored	신신하다	sim sim ha da
boring	지루하다, 지루한	ji ru ha da, ji ru han
born, to be	대이나다	tae-eo na da
borrow, to	빌리다	bil li da
botanic gardens	식물원	sing mu rwon
both	둘 다	dul da
bottle (baby's)	젖병	jeot byeong
bottle (wine)	술병	sul ppyeong
bottle-warmer	젖병 보온기	jeot byeong bo on-gi
box	상자	sang ja
box office	매표소	mae pyo so
boy	소년	so-nyeon
boyfriend	남자 친구	nam ja chin-gu
bra	브래지어	beu rae ji eo
bracelet	팔찌	pal jji
brake	브레이크	beu re i keu
brake oil	브레이크 오일	beu re i keu oil
bread	빵	ppang

break, shatter, to	깨뜨리다	kkae tteu ri da
breakfast, morning meal	아침 식사	a chim sik sa
breast milk	모유	mo yu
breasts	가슴	ga seum
bridge	다리	da ri
briefs	팬티	paen ti
bring, to	가져오다	ga jyeo-o da
brochure	브로셔	beu ro syeo
broken (of bones, etc.)	부러지다, 부러진	bu reo ji da, bu reo jin
broken, does not work	고장나다/-난	go jang na da, go jang nan
bronze	청동	cheong dong
broth, soup	국	guk
brother	형제	hyeong je
brown	갈색(의)	gal saek(ui)
bruise	멍	meong
brush	솔, 붓	sol, but
bucket	양동이	yang dong-i
Buddhism	불교	bul gyo
buffet	뷔페	bwi pe
bugs	벌레	beol le
building	빌딩	bil ding
bun	롤빵	rol ppang
burglary	도난, 강도	do nan, gang do
burn (injury)	화상	hwa sang
burn, to	태우다, 타다	tae-u da, ta da
bus	버스	beo seu
bus station	버스 정거장	beo seu jeong geo jang
bus stop	버스 정류장	beo seu jeong nyu jang
business card	명함	myeong ham
business class	비지니스 클라스	bi ji ni s keul la s
business trip	출장	chul jang
busy (schedule)	바쁘다, 바쁜	ba ppeu da, ba ppeun
busy (traffic)	복잡하다, 복잡한	bok jap ha da, bok ja pan
but	그러나, -지만	geu reo na, -ji man
butane	부탄가스	bu tan ga seu
butchers	정육점	jeong yuk jeom
butter	버터	beo teo
button	단추	dan chu
buy, to	사다	sa da
by airmail	항공우편으로	hang gong-u pyeo neu ro
by phone	전화로	jeon hwa ro

C

cabbage	양배추	yang bae chu
cabbage, Chinese	배추	bae chu
cabin (boat)	선실	seon sil
cake, pastry	케이크	ke i keu
call (phone call)	전화	jeon hwa
call, phone, to	전화하다	jeon hwa ha da
called, named	불리다, 불리는	bul li da, bul li neun
camera	카메라	ka me ra
camera memory	카메라 메모리	ka me ra me mo ri
camping	캠핑	kaem ping
can opener	깡통 따개	kkang tong tta gae
can, be able to	-(으)ㄹ 수 있다	-(eu)l su it da
can, may	-아/어도 좋다/되다	-a/eo do jo ta/doe da

cancel, to	취소하다	chwi so ha da
candle	양초	yang cho
candy, sweets	사탕	sa tang
cap	모자	mo ja
capable of, to be	- (으)ㄹ 수 있다	-(eu)l su it da
car, automobile	자동차	ja dong cha
car documents	차량 등록증	cha ryang deung nok jeung
car seat (child's)	어린이 보호 좌석	eo ri ni bo ho jwa seok
car trouble	차량 고장	cha ryang go jang
cardigan	카디간	ka di gan
careful!	조심하세요!	jo sim ha se yo!
carpet	카페트	ka pe teu
carriage, pram	유모차	yu mo cha
carrot	당근	dang geun
cartridge	카트릿지	ka teu rit ji
cash, money	현금	hyeon-geum
cash card	현금 카드	hyeon-geum ka deu
cash desk	계산대	gye san dae
cash machine	현금 지급기	hyeon-geum ji geup gi
casino	카지노	ka ji no
cassette	카세트	ka se teu
cat	고양이	go yang-i
catalogue	카달로그	ka dal lo geu
cauliflower	컬리플라워	keol li peul la wo
cause	원인	wo nin
cave	동굴	dong gul
CD	씨디	ssi di
CD-ROM	씨디-롬	ssi di-rom
celebrate, to	축하하다	chuk ha ha da
cemetery	공동묘지	gong dong myo ji
centimetre	센티미터	sen ti mi teo
central heating	중앙 난방	jung-ang nan bang
central locking	중앙 잠금 장치	jung-ang jang geum jang chi
center (middle)	중앙, 가운데	jung-ang, ga un de
center (of city)	(시내) 중심지	(si nae) jung sim ji
certificate	증명서	jeung myeong seo
chair	의자	ui ja
chambermaid	메이드	me i deu
champagne	샴페인	syam pe in
change (money)	잔돈	jan don
change (trains)	바꿔타다	ba kkwo ta da
change the baby's diaper/nappy	기저귀를 갈다	gi jeo-gwi reul gal da
change the oil	오일을 갈다	o i reul gal da
change, exchange (money), to	환전하다	hwan jeon ha da
change, swap, to	바꾸다	ba kku da
charter flight	전세기 편	jeon se gi pyeon
chat, to	이야기하다	i ya gi ha da
cheap	싸다, 싼	ssa da, ssan
check in	체크인하다	che keu-in ha da
check out	체크아웃하다	che keu a ut ha da
check, cheque	수표	su pyo
check, verify, to	체크하다	che keu ha da
checked luggage	체크한 여행가방	che keu han yeo haeng ga bang

cheers!	건배!	geon bae!
cheese	치즈	chi jeu
chef	요리사	yo ri sa
chess	체스	che seu
chewing gum	껌	kkeom
chicken	닭(고기)	dak(go gi)
child	아이/애, 어린이	a i/ae, eo ri ni
child's seat (in car)	어린이 보호 좌석	eo ri ni bo ho jwa seok
chilli paste	고추장	go chu jang
chin	턱	teok
China	중국	jung guk
chocolate	초콜렛	cho kol let
choose, to	선택하다	seon taek ha da
chopsticks	젓가락	jeot ga rak
Christianity	기독교	gi dok gyo
church	교회	gyo hoe
church service	예배	ye bae
cigar	시가	si ga
cigarette	담배	dam bae
cinema	극장	geuk jang
circus	서커스	seo keo seu
citizen	시민	si min
city	도시	do si
clean	깨끗하다, 깨끗한	kkae kkeut ha da, kkae kkeu tan
clean, to	청소하다	cheong so ha da
clearance (sale)	세일	se il
climate	기후	gi hu
clock	시계	si gye
closed (shop)	끝나다, 끝난	kkeun na da, kkeun nan
closed off (road)	(도로가) 차단되다	(do ro ga) cha dan doe da
cloth	옷감	ot gam
clothes dryer	건조기	geon jo gi
clothes hanger	옷걸이	ot geo ri
clothes, clothing	옷	ot
cloudy, overcast	흐리다, 흐린	heu ri da, heu rin
clutch (car)	클러치	keul leo chi
coat, overcoat	코트	ko teu
cockroach	바퀴벌레	ba kwi beol le
cocoa	코코아	ko ko a
coffee	커피	keo pi
coin	동전	dong jeon
cold (not hot)	춥다, 추운	chup da, chu un
cold, flu	감기	gam gi
collar	칼라	kal la
collarbone	쇄골	swae gol
colleague, co-worker	동료	dong nyo
collide, to	충돌하다	chung dol ha da
collision	충돌	chung dol
cologne	화장수	hwa jang su
color	색	saek
comb	빗	bit
come, to	오다	o da
company, firm	회사	hoe sa
compartment	칸	kan
complaint	불평	bul pyeong
completely	완전히	wan jeon hi

compliment	칭찬	ching chan
computer	컴퓨터	keom pyu teo
computer game	컴퓨터 게임	keom pyu teo ge im/ com pu ter ge im
concert	콘서트	kon seo teu
concert hall	콘서트 홀	kon seo teu hol
concierge	수위	su wi
concussion	뇌진탕	noe jin tang
condensed milk	연유	yeo nyu
condom	콘돔	kon dom
confectionery	과자	gwa ja
congratulations!	축하해요!	chuk ha hae yo!
connection (transport)	연결편	yeon-gyeol pyeon
constipation	변비	byeon bi
consulate	영사관	yeong sa.gwan
consultation (by doctor)	진찰	jin chal
contact lens	콘택트 렌즈	kon taek teu ren jeu
contagious	전염되다, 전염되는	jeon yeom doe da, jeon yeom doe neun
contraceptive	피임	pi im
contraceptive pill	피임약	pi im yak
cook (person)	요리사	yo ri sa
cook, to	요리하다	yo ri ha da
cookie, sweet biscuit	쿠키	ku ki
copper	구리	gu ri
copy	사본, 복사	sa bon, bok sa
copy, to	복사하다	bok sa ha da
corkscrew	코르크 따개	ko reu keu tta gae
corner	코너	ko neo
cornflower	옥수수 가루	ok su su ga ru
correct, to	고치다	go chi da
correspond (letters), to	편지 연락하다	pyeon ji yeol lak ha da
corridor	복도	bok do
cosmetics	화장품	hwa jang pum
costume	의상	ui sang
cotton	면	myeon
cotton wool	솜	som
cough	기침	gi chim
cough syrup	기침 물약	gi chim mul lyak
cough, to	기침하다	gi chim ha da
counter (for paying, buying tickets)	키오트	ka un teu
country (nation)	나라	na ra
country (rural area)	시골	si gol
country code	국가 번호	guk ga beon ho
courgettes, zucchini	(애)호박	(ae)ho bak
course of treatment	치료	chi ryo
cousin	사촌	sa chon
crab	게	ge
cracker, salty biscuit	크래커	keu rae keo
cream	크림	keu rim
credit card	신용카드	si nyong ka deu
cot, crib	아기 침대	a gi chim dae
crime	범죄	beom joe
crockery	그릇	geu reut
cross, angry	화나다, 화난	hwa na da, hwa nan
cross (road, river), to	건너다	geon neo da

crossroad	교차로	gyo cha ro
crosswalk, pedestrian crossing	건널목	geon neol mok
crutch	목발	mok bal
cry, to	울다	ul da
cubic metre	입방미터	ip bang mi teo
cucumber	오이	o i
cuddly toy	동물 인형	dong mul in hyeong
cuffs	소매단	so mae dan
cup	컵	keop
curly	곱슬하다/-한	gop seul ha da/-han
current (electric)	전류	jeol lyu
curtains	커튼	keo teun
cushion	쿠션	ku syeon
custom (tradition)	관습	gwan seup
customs	세관	se gwan
cut (injury)	상처	sang cheo
cut, to	자르다	ja reu da
cutlery	포크, 나이프, 스푼	po keu, na i peu, seu pun
cycling	자전거 타기	ja jeon-geo ta gi
Cyworld	싸이월드	ssa i wol deu/Cyworld

D

dairy products	유제품	yu je pum
damage	손해, 손상	son hae, son sang
dance	춤	chum
dance, to	춤추다	chum chu da
dandruff	비듬	bi deum
danger	위험	wi heom
dangerous	위험하다, 위험한	wi heom ha da, wi heom han
dark	어둡다/진하다, 어두운/진한	eo dup da/jin ha da, eo du un/jin han
date (of the month)	날짜	nal jja
date of birth	생년월일	saeng nyeo nwo ril
daughter	딸	ttal
day	날, 낮	nal, nat
day after tomorrow	모레	mo re
day before yesterday	그저께	geu jeo kke
dead	죽다, 죽은	juk da, ju geun
deaf	귀가 먹다/먹은	gwi ga meok da/meo geun
decaffeinated	카페인 없는	ka pe in eom neun
December	십이월	si bi wol
declare (customs)	신고	sin-go
deep	깊다, 깊은	gip da, gip eun
deep freeze, freezer	냉동고	naeng dong go
deep-sea diving	스킨 다이빙	seu kin da i bing
defecate, to	배설하다	bae seol ha da
degrees (temperature)	도	do
delay	지연	ji yeon
delete, to	삭제하다, 지우다	sak je ha da, ji u da
delicious	맛있다, 맛있는	ma sit da, ma sin neun
dentist	치과(의사)	chi kkwa(ui sa)
dentures	틀니	teul li
deodorant	탈취제	tal chwi je
department store	백화점	baek hwa jeom
departure	출발	chul bal

depilatory cream	탈모제	tal mo je
deposit (for safekeeping), to	보관하다	bo-gwan ha da
deposit (in the bank), to	예금하다	ye geum ha da
desert (arid land)	사막	sa mak
dessert	디저트	di jeo teu
destination	목적지	mok jeok ji
detergent	세제	se je
develop (film), to	현상하다	hyeon sang ha da
diabetic	당뇨병 환자	dang nyo byeong hwan ja
dial (telephone), to	전화하다	jeon hwa ha da
diamond	다이아몬드	da i a mon deu
diaper	기저귀	go jeo-gwi
diarrhoea	설사	seol sa
dictionary	사전	sa jeon
diesel oil	디젤유	di jel lyu
diet	식이요법	si gi yo beop
difficulty	어려움	eo ryeo um
dining car	식당칸	sik dang kan
dining room	식당	sik dang
dinner, evening meal	저녁 식사	jeo nyeok sik sa
direct flight	직항	jik hang
direction	방향	bang hyang
directly	직접	jik jeop
dirty	더럽다, 더러운	deo reop da, deo reo.un
disabled person	장애인	jang-ae In
discount	디스카운트	di seu ka un teu
discuss, to	의논하다	ui non ha da
discussion	의논	ui non
dish (particular food)	요리	yo ri
dish of the day	오늘의 스페셜	o neu rui seu pe syeol
disinfectant	소독제	so dok je
dislike, to	싫어하다	si reo ha da
distance	거리	geo ri
distilled water	증류수	jeung nyu su
disturb, to	방해하다	bang hae ha da
disturbance	방해	bang hae
dive, to	다이빙하다	da i bing ha da
diving	다이빙	da i bing
diving board	다이빙 보드	da i bing bo deu
diving gear	다이빙 장비	da i bing jang bi
divorced	이혼하다, 이혼한	i hon ha da, i hon han
dizzy	어지럽다, 어지러운	eo ji reop da, eo ji reo un
do not disturb	방해하지 마세요.	bang hae ha ji ma se yo.
do, perform an action, to	하다	ha da
doctor	의사	ui sa
dog	개	gae
doll	인형	in hyeong
domestic (flight)	국내선	gung nae seon
don't!	그러지 마세요!	geu reo ji ma se yo!
done (cooked)	잘 익다, 잘 익은	jal ik da, jal i geun
door	문	mun
double	두 배	du bae
down, downward	아래로	a rae ro
drapes, curtains	커튼	keo teun
dream, to	꿈꾸다	kkum kku da
dress, frock	드레스	deu re seu
dressing gown	실내복	sil lae bok

dressing table	화장대	hwa jang dae
drink (alcoholic)	술	sul
drink (refreshment)	음료(수)	eum nyo(su)
drink, to	마시다	ma si da
drinking water	식수	sik su
drive (a car), to	운전하다	un jeon ha da
driver	운전사	un jeon sa
driver's license	운전 면허증	un jeon myeon heo jjeung
drugstore, pharmacy	약국	yak guk
drunk	술 취하다	sul chwi ha da
dry	마르다, 마른	ma reu da, ma reun
dry, to	말리다	mal li da
dry-clean	드라이 클리닝	deu ra i keul li ning
dry cleaners	세탁소	se tak so
duck	오리	o ri
during, for	...동안	...dong-an
duty (import tax)	관세	gwan se
duty-free goods	면세품	myeon se pum
duty-free shop	면세점	myeon se jeom
DVD	디비디	di bi di

E

ear	귀	gwi
ear drops	귀 물약	gwi mul lyak
earache	이통	i tong
early	이르다, 이른	i reu da, i reun
earrings	귀걸이	gwi geo ri
earth, soil	흙	heuk
earthenware	도기	do gi
east	동쪽	dong jjok
easy	쉽다, 쉬운	swip da, swi un
eat, to	먹다	meok da
economy class	이코노미석	i ko no mi seok
eczema	습진	seup jin
eel	장어	jang-eo
egg	계란, 알	gye ran, al
eggplant, aubergine	가지	gaji
electric	전기(의)	jeon-gi(ui)
electricity	전기	jeon-gi
electronic	전자(의)	jeon ja(ui)
elephant	코끼리	ko kki ri
elevator	엘리베이터	el li be i teo
email (message)	이메일	i me il/email
email address	이메일 주소	i me il ju so/email ju so
embassy	대사관	dae sa gwan
embroidery	(자)수	(ja)su
emergency	응급(사태)	eung geup(sa tae)
emergency brake	비상 브레이크	bi sang beu re i keu
emergency exit	비상구	bi sang gu
emergency phone	응급 전화	eung geup jeon hwa
emergency room	응급실	eung geup sil
empty	텅 비다/빈	teong bi da/bin
engaged (telephone)	통화중이다/-중인	tong hwa jung-i da/ -jung-in
engaged (to be married)	약혼하다/-한	ya kon ha da/-han
England	영국	yeong guk

English	영어	yeong-eo
enjoy, to	즐기다	jeul gi da
enquire, to	물어보다	mu reo bo da
envelope	봉투	bong tu
escalator	에스컬레이터	e seu keol le i teo
essential	필수적이다, 필수적인	pil su jeo gi da, pil su jeo gin

evening	저녁	jeo nyeok
evening wear	야회복	ya hoe bok
event	행사	haeng sa
every	모든, 매...	mo deun, mae...
everybody, everyone	모든 사람	mo deun sa ram
everything	모든 것	mo deun geot
everywhere	어디든지, 모든 곳	eo di deun ji, mo deun got

| examine, to | 검토하다, 진찰하다 | geom to ha da, jin chal ha da |

excavation	발굴	bal gul
excellent	우수하다, 우수한	u su ha da, u su han
exchange (money, opinions), to	교환하다	gyo hwan ha da
exchange office	환전소	hwan jeon so
exchange rate	환율	hwan nyul
excuse me!	실례합니다!	sil lye ham ni da!
excuse me! (apology)	미안합니다!	mi an ham ni da!
exhibition	전시회	jeon si hoe
exit, way out	출구	chul gu
expense	비용	bi yong
expensive	비싸다, 비싼	bi ssa da, bi ssan
explain, to	설명하다	seol myeong ha da
express, state, to	표현하다	pyo hyeon ha da
eye	눈	nun
eye drops	눈약	nun yak
eye specialist	안과 전문의	an kkwa jeon mun-ui

F

fabric, textile	직물	jing mul
face	얼굴	eol gul
Facebook	페이스북	pe i seu buk/Facebook
factory	공장	gong jang
fall (season)	가을	ga-eul
fall over, to	넘어지다	neo meo ji da
family	가족	ga jok
famous	유명하다, 유명한	yu myeong ha da, yu myeong han

fan (admirer)	팬	paen
fan (for cooling)	부채	bu chae
far away	멀다, 먼	meol da, meon
farm	농장	nong jang
farmer	농부	nong bu
fashion	패션	pae syeon
fast, rapid	빠르다, 빠른	ppa reu da, ppa reun
father	아버지	a beo ji
father-in-law	시아버지, 장인	si a beo ji, jang.in
fault	잘못	jal mot
fax	팩스	paek seu
fax, to	팩스 보내다	paek seu bo nae da
February	이월	i wol

feel like	-고 싶다	-go sip da
feel, to	느끼다	neu kki da
female	여성	yeo seong
fence	담, 울타리	dam, ul ta ri
ferry	배	bae
fever	열	yeol
fiancé	약혼자	ya kon ja
fiancée	약혼녀	ya kon nyeo
fill out (form), to	작성하다	jak seong ha da
fill, to	채우다	chae.u da
film (camera)	필름	pil leum
filter	필터	pil teo
fine (good)	좋다, 좋은	jo ta, jo-eun
fine (money)	벌금	beol geum
finger	손가락	son kka rak
fire	불	bul
fire alarm	화재 경보	hwa jae gyeong bo
fire department, fire service	소방서	so bang seo
fire escape	비상구	bi sang gu
fire extinguisher	소화기	so hwa gi
first	첫 번째	cheot beon jjae
first aid	응급 조치	eung geup jo chi
first class	일등석	il deung seok
fish	물고기, 생선	mul kko gi (*live*), saeng seon (*food*)
fishing	낚시	nak si
fishing rod	낚싯대	nak sit dae
fitness club	헬스 클럽	hel seu keul leop
fitness training	체력 단련	che ryeok dal lyeon
fitting room	탈의실	ta rui sil
fix (repair), to	고치다	go chi da
flag	깃발	git bal
flash (camera)	플래쉬	peul lae swi
flashlight, torch	손전등	son jeon deung
flatulence	복부 팽만	bok bu paeng man
flavor	맛	mat
flavoring	첨가물	cheom ga mul
flea	벼룩	byeo ruk
flea market	벼룩시장	byeo ruk si jang
flight	운항	un hang
flight number	운항 번호	un hang beon ho
flood	홍수	hong su
floor	마루, 층	ma ru, cheung
flour	밀가루	mil kka ru
flower	꽃	kkot
flu	독감	dok gam
flush (toilet), to	변기 물을 내리다	byeon.gi mu reul nae ri da
fly (insect)	파리	pa ri
fly, to	날다	nal da
fog	안개	an.gae
foggy	안개끼다, 안개낀	an.gae kki da, an.gae kkin
folklore	민담	min dam
follow behind, to	뒤따라가다	dwi tta ra ga da
food (meal)	음식	eum sik
food court	음식 백화점	eum sik baek hwa jeom
food poisoning	식중독	sik jung dok

foot	발	bal
foot brake	발 브레이크	bal beu re i keu
forbidden	금지되다, 금지된	geum ji doe da, geum ji doen
forehead	이마	i ma
foreign	외국(의)	oe guk(ui)
foreigner	외국인	oe gu gin
forget, to	잊어버리다	i jeo beo ri da
fork	포크	po keu
form (application)	신청서	sin cheong seo
form (to fill out), to	작성하다	jak seong ha da
formal dress	정장	jeong jang
fountain	분수	bun su
frame (photo)	액자	aek ja
free (no charge)	무료(의)	mu ryo(ui)
free (unoccupied)	비어있다, 비어있는	bi eo-it da, bi eo-in neun
free time	자유시간	ja yu si gan
freeze, to	얼(리)다	eol(li) da
french fries	감자 튀김	gam ja twi gim
fresh	신선하다, 신선한	sin seon ha da, sin seon han
Friday	금요일	geu myo il
fried	튀긴	twi gin
friend	친구	chin.gu
friendly	친절하다, 친절한	chin jeol ha da, chin jeol han
frightened	겁먹다, 겁먹은	geom meok da, geom meo geun
fringe (hair)	앞머리	am meo ri
frozen	얼다, 언	eol da, eon
fruit	과일	gwa il
fruit juice	과일 주스	gwa il ju seu
frying pan	프라이펜	peu ra i paen
full	가득 차다/찬	ga deuk cha da, ga deuk chan
fun, to have	재미있게 보내다	jae mi it ge bo nae da
funeral	장례식	jang nye sik

G

gallery	화랑	hwa rang
game	게임	ge im
garage (for repairs)	정비소	jeong bi so
garbage	쓰레기	sseu re gi
garden, yard	정원	jeong-won
garlic	마늘	ma neul
garment	옷	ot
gas (for heating)	가스	ga seu
gas station	주유소	ju yu so
gasoline	가솔린	ga sol lin
gasoline station	주유소	ju yu so
gate	문	mun
gear (car)	기어	gi eo
gem	보석	bo seok
gender	성별	seong byeol
genuine	진짜(의)	jin jja(ui)
germ	세균	se-gyun
get off (transport), to	내리다	nae ri da

get on (transport) , to	타다	ta da
gift	선물	seon mul
ginger	생강	saeng gang
girl	소녀	so.nyeo
girlfriend	여자 친구	yeo ja chin-gu
give, to	주다	ju da
given name	이름	i reum
glad	기쁘다, 기쁜	gi ppeu da, gi ppeun
glass (for drinking)	컵	keop
glass (material)	유리	yu ri
glasses, spectacles	안경	an-gyeong
gliding	글라이딩	geul la i ding
glossy (photo)	광택지	gwang taek ji
gloves	장갑	jang gap
glue	풀	pul
gnat	모기	mo gi
go back , to	돌아가다	do ra ga da
go out, exit, to	나가다	na ga da
go to bed, to	자다/자러가다	ja da/ja reo ga da
go, to	가다	ga da
gold	금	geum
golf	골프	gol peu
golf course	골프장	gol peu jang
good	좋다, 좋은	jo ta, jo-eun
good afternoon	안녕하세요.	an nyeong ha se yo
good evening	안녕하세요.	an nyeong ha se yo
good luck!	행운을 빕니다!	haeng-u neul bim ni da!
good morning	안녕하세요.	an nyeong ha se yo
good night	안녕히 주무세요.	an nyeong hi ju mu se yo
goodbye (to a person leaving)	안녕히 가세요	an nyeong hi ga se yo
goodbye (to a person staying)	안녕히 계세요	an nyeong hi gye se yo
grade crossing, level crossing	철도 건널목	cheol do geon neol mok
gram	그램	g raem
grammar	문법	mun beop
grandchild	손자(M), 손녀(F)	son ja (M), son nyeo (F)
granddaughter	손녀	son nyeo
grandfather	할아버지, 조부	ha ra beo ji, jo bu
grandmother	할머니, 조모	hal meo ni, jo mo
grandparents	조부모	jo bu mo
grandson	손자	son ja
grape juice	포도 주스	po do ju seu
grapes	포도	po do
grave	무덤	mu deom
graze (injury)	찰과상	chal gwa sang
greasy	기름기 많다, 기름기 많은	gi reum kki man ta, gi reum kki ma neun
green	푸르다, 푸른	pu reu da, pu reun
greengrocer	야채	ya chae
greet, to	인사하다	in sa ha da
greetings	인사말	in sa mal
grey	회색(의)	hoe saek(ui)
grey-haired	백발의	baek ba rui
grilled	굽다, 구운	gup da, gu un
grocery	식품점	sik pum jeom
groceries	식품	sik pum
group	그룹	geu rup
guest	손님	son nim

English	Korean	Romanization
guest house	여관	yeo gwan
guide (book)	안내서	an nae seo
guide (person)	가이드	ga i deu
guided tour	가이드가 있는 투어	ga i deu ga in neun tu eo
guilty, to feel	죄책감을 느끼다	joe chaek ga meul neu kki da
gym	짐	jim
gynaecologist	산부인과 의사	san bu-in kkwa ui sa

H

English	Korean	Romanization
hair	머리(카락)	meo ri(ka rak)
hairbrush	빗	bit
haircut	컷트	keo teu
hairdresser	미용사	mi yong sa
hair dryer	헤어 드라이어	he-eo deu ra i eo
hair spray	헤어 스프레이	he-eo seu peu rei
hair style	헤어 스타일	he-eo seu ta il
half	반	ban
half full	반	ban
hammer	망치	mang chi
hand	손	son
hand brake	손 브레이크	son beu re i keu
hand luggage	휴대 수하물	hyu dae su ha mul
hand towel	손 타월	son ta wol
handbag	핸드백	haen deu baek
handkerchief	손수건	son su geon
handmade	수공	su gong
happy	행복하나, 행복한	haeng bok ha da, hang bo kan
happy birthday!	생일 축하합니다!	saeng-il chuk ha ham ni da!
happy new year!	새해 복 많이 받으세요!	sae hae bok ma ni ba deu se yo!
harbor	항구	hang gu
hard (difficult)	어렵다, 어려운	eo ryeop da, eo ryeo-un
hard (firm)	단단하다, 단단한	dan dan ha da, dan dan han
hardware	하드웨어	ha deu we eo/hardware
hardware store	철물점	cheol mul jeom
hat	모자	mo ja
have to, must	-아/어야 하다	-a/eo ya ha da
have, own, to	있다	it da
hay fever	꽃가루 알레르기	kkot ga ru al le reu gi
he, him	그	geu
head	머리	meo ri
headache	두통	du tong
headlights	헤드 라이트	he deu ra i teu
health food shop	건강 식품점	geon-gang sik pum jeom
healthy	건강하다, 건강한	geon-gang ha da, geon-gang han
hear, to	듣다	deut da
hearing aid	보청기	bo cheong gi
heart	심장, 마음	sim jang, ma-eum
heart attack	심장 마비	sim jang ma bi
heat, to	데우다	de-u da
heater	히터	hi teo
heavy	무겁다, 무거운	mu geop da, mu geo.un

heel (of foot)	발꿈치	bal kkum chi
heel (of shoe)	굽	gup
hello! (on phone)	여보세요!	yeo bo se yo!
hello, hi	안녕하세요	an nyeong ha se yo
help!	도와주세요!	do wa ju se yo!
help yourself	마음대로 드세요	ma-eum dae ro deu se yo
hem	단	dan
her	그녀의	geu nyeo.ui
herbal tea	허브 차	heo beu cha
herbs	허브	heo beu
here	여기, 이리(로)	yeo gi, i ri(ro)
hers	그녀의 것	geu nyeo-ui geot
high	높다, 높은	nop da, no peun
high tide	밀물	mil mul
highway	고속도로	go sok do ro
hiking	등산	deung san
hiking boots	등산화	deung san hwa
hip	힙	hip
hire, to	고용하다	go yong ha da
his	그의, 그의 것	geu-ui, geu-ui geot
hitchhike	히치 하이크	hi chi ha i keu
hobby	취미	chwi mi
holiday (public)	휴일	hyu-il
holiday (vacation)	휴가	hyu ga
home, house	집	jip
homesickness	향수병	hyang su ppyeong
honest	정직하다, 정직한	jeong jik ha da, jeong ji kan
honey	꿀	kkul
horizontal	수평이다, 수평인	su pyeong-ida, supyeong-in
horrible	형편없다, 형편없는	hyeong pyeo neop da, hyeong pyeo neom neun
horse	말	mal
hospital	병원	byeong-won
hospitality (friendly)	환대	hwan dae
hot (spicy)	맵다, 매운	maep da, mae-un
hot (temperature)	덥다, 더운	deop da, deo-un
hot spring	온천	on cheon
hot-water bottle	보온병	bo on byeong
hotel	호텔	ho tel
hour	시간	si gan
house	집	jip
how are you?	안녕하세요?	an nyeong ha se yo?
how far?	얼마나 멀어요	eol ma na meo reo yo?
how long?	얼마나 오래요?	eol ma na o rae yo?
how many?	얼마나 많이요?	eol ma na ma ni yo?
how much?	얼마예요?	eol ma ye yo?
how old?	몇 살이에요?	myeot sa ri e yo?
how?	어떻게요?	eo tteo ke yo?
however	그러나	geu reo na
humid	무덥다, 무더운	mu deop da, mu deo.un
hundred grams	백 그램	baek geu raem
hungry	배고프다, 배고픈	bae go peu da, bae go peun
hurry up!	빨리요!	ppal li yo!
husband	남편	nam pyeon

hut, shack	오두막	o du mak

I

I, me	나, 내, 저, 제	na, nae, jeo, je
ice cream	아이스 크림	a i seu keu rim
ice cubes	얼음 조각	eo reum jo gak
ice-skating	아이스 스케이팅	a i seu seu ke i ting
iced	얼다, 언	eol da, eon
idea	생각	saeng gak
identification (card)	신분증	sin bun jjeung
if	만일 -(으)면	ma nil -(eu)myeon
ignition key	차 열쇠	cha yeol soe
ill, sick	아프다, 아픈	a peu da, a peun
illness	병	byeong
imagine, to	상상하다	sang sang ha da
immediately	곧	got
import duty	관세	gwan se
important	중요하다, 중요한	jung-yo ha da, jung-yo han
impossible	불가능하다/- 한	bul ga neung ha da/-han
in order that, so that	-기 위해서	-gi wi hae seo
in the evening	저녁에	jeo-nyeo ge
in the morning	아침에	a chi me
in, at (place)	...에(서)	...e(seo)
in-laws	처가 사람, 시대 사람	cheo ga sa ram, si daek sa ram
included	포함되다, 포함된	po ham doe da, po ham doen
including	포함하다, 포함하는	po ham ha da, po ham ha neun
indicate, to	가리키다	ga ri ki da
indicator (car)	깜박이 등	kkam ba gi deung
indigestion	소화불량	so hwa bul lyang
inexpensive	싸다, 싼	ssa da, ssan
infection	감염	ga myeom
infectious	전염되다, 전염되는	jeo nyeom doe da, jeo nyeom doe nuen
inflammation	염증	yeom jjeung
information	정보, 안내	jeong bo, an nae
information office	안내소	an nae so
injection	주사	ju sa
injured	나치나, 다친	da chi da, da chin
innocent	결백하다, 결백한	gyeol bae ka da, gyeol bae kan
insane	미치다, 미친	mi chi da, mi chin
insect	벌레	beol le
insect bite	벌레 물린 상처	beol le mul lin sang cheo
insect repellent	방충제	bang chung je
inside	안	an jjok
instructions	사용 설명서	sa yong seol myeong seo
insurance	보험	bo heom
interested in	관심이 있다/ 있는	gwan si mi it da/in neun
interesting	재미있다, 재미있는	jae mi it da, jae mi in neun
intermission	중간 휴식	jung gan hyu sik
internal	내부의	nae bu ui

Internet	인터넷	in teo net/Internet
Internet café	인터넷 카페	in teo net ka pe
interpreter	통역(사)	tong-yeok(sa)
intersection	교차(로)	gyo cha(ro)
interview	면접	myeon jeop
introduce someone, to	소개하다	so gae ha da
invent, to	발명하다	bal myeong ha da
invite, to	초대하다	cho dae ha da
invoice	청구서	cheong gu seo
iodine	요오드	yo o deu
I-Pad	아이패드	a i pae deu/I-Pad
I-phone	아이폰	a i pon/I-phone
Ireland	아일랜드	a il laen deu
iron (metal)	철	cheol
iron (clothing), to	다리다	da ri da
ironing board	다림질판	da rim jil pan
island	섬	seom
itch	가려움증	ga ryeo um jjeung

J

jack (for car)	잭	jaek
jacket	자켓	ja ket
jam	잼	jaem
January	일월	i rwol
Japan	일본	il bon
jaw	턱	teok
jeans	진	jin
jellyfish	해파리	hae pa ri
jeweller	보석상	bo seok sang
jewellery	보석	bo seok
job	직업, 일	ji geop, il
jog, to	조깅하다	jo ging ha da
joke	농담	nong dam
journey	여행	yeo haeng
juice	쥬스	jyu seu
July	칠월	chi rwol
June	유월	yu wol

K

kerosene	등유	deung yu
key (to room)	열쇠	yeol soe
kidney	신장	sin jang
kilogram	킬로그램	kil lo geu raem
king	왕	wang
kiss	키스	ki seu
kiss, to	키스하다	ki seu ha da
kitchen	부엌	bu-eok
knee	무릎	mu reup
knife	칼	kal
knit	니트	ni teu
know, to	알다	al da
Korea, North	북한	buk han
Korea, South	남한	nam han
Korean	한국 사람, 한국어	han-guk sa ram, han-gu geo
Korean drama	한국 드라마	han guk deu ra ma/ han guk d ra ma

Korean Pop	한국 대중음악	han guk dae jung eu mak

L

lace (fabric)	레이스	re i seu
laces (for shoes)	신발 끈	sin bal kkeun
ladder	사다리	sa da ri
lake	호수	ho su
lamb, mutton	양고기	yang go gi
lamp	등	deung
land (ground)	땅	ttang
land (plane), to	착륙하다	chang nyuk ha da
lane (of traffic)	차선	cha seon
language	말, 언어	mal, eo neo
large	크다, 큰	keu da, keun
last (endure)	오래가다	o rae ga da
last (final)	마지막이다, 마지막	ma ji ma gi da, ma ji mak
last night	지난 밤	ji nan bam
later	나중에	na jung-e
laugh, to	웃다	ut da
launderette	빨래방	ppal lae bang
laundry	세탁소	se tak so
law, legislation	법	beop
lawyer	변호사	byeon ho sa
laxative	완화제	wan hwa je
leak, to	새다	sae da
leather	가죽	ga juk
leather goods	가죽 제품	ga juk je pum
leave, depart, to	떠나다	tteo na da
left behind	남다	nam da
left-hand side	왼쪽	oen jjok
leg	다리	da ri
leggings	레깅즈	re ging jeu
leisure	레저	re jeo
lemon, citrus	레몬	re mon
lend, to	빌려주다	bil lyeo ju da
lens (camera)	렌즈	ren jeu
less (smaller amount)	더 적다/적은	deo jeok da/jeo geun
lesson	수업, 강습	su-eop, gang seup
letter	편지	pyeon ji
lettuce	양상치	yang sang chi
level crossing, grade crossing	철도 건널목	cheol do geon neol mok
library	도서관	do seo gwan
license (for driving)	면허증	myeon heo jjeung
lie (falsehood)	거짓말	geo jin mal
lie down, to	눕다	nup da
lift (elevator)	엘리베이터	el li be i teo
lift (in car), to give	태워주다	tae wo ju da
light (lamp)	불	bul
light (not dark)	밝다/연하다, 밝은/연한	bal tta/yeon ha da, bal geun/yeon han
light (not heavy)	가볍다, 가벼운	ga byeop da, ga byeo.un
light bulb	전구	jeon gu
lighter	라이터	ra i teo
lightning	번개	beon.gae
like, be pleased by, to	좋아하다	jo a ha da
line (mark)	선	seon
line (queue)	줄	jul

linen (fiber)	린넨	rin nen
lining	안감	an kkam
liquor store	주류상	ju ryu sang
liquor, alcohol	술	sul
listen, to	듣다	deut da
literature	문학	mun hak
litre	리터	ri teo
little (amount)	적다, 적은	jeok da, jeo geun
little (small)	작다, 작은	jak da, ja geun
live (be alive)	살아있는	sa ra in neun
live, to	살다	sal da
liver	간	gan
lobster	롭스터	rop seu teo
local	지역	ji yeok
lock	자물쇠	ja mul soe
long (length)	길다, 긴	gil da, gin
look at, see, to	보다	bo da
look for, to	찾다	chat da
look up (find in book), to	찾아보다	cha ja bo da
lose, mislay, to	잃어버리다	i reo beo ri da
loss (profit)	손실	son sil
lost (can't find way)	길을 잃다/잃은	gi reul il ta/i reun
lost (missing)	잃어버린	i reo beo rin
lost and found office	분실물 센터	bun sil mul sen teo
lotion	로션	ro syeon
loud	소리가 크다/큰	so ri ga keu da/keun
love	사랑	sa rang
love, to	사랑하다	sarang ha da
low	낮다, 낮은	nat da, na jeun
low tide	썰물	sseol mul
LPG	엘피지	el pi ji
luck	운	un
luggage	여행가방	yeo haeng ga bang
luggage locker	보관함	bo gwan ham
lumps (sugar)	각설탕	gak seol tang
lunch	점심 식사	jeom sim sik sa
lungs	폐	pye

M

madam (term of address)	부인	bu.in
magazine	잡지	jap ji
mail, post	우편물	u pyeon mul
mail, to	부치다	bu chi da
main post office	중앙 우체국	jung-ang u che guk
main road	대로	dae ro
make an appointment	약속하다	yak sok ha da
make love	섹스하다	sek seu ha da
make, create, to	만들다	man deul da
makeshift	임시	im si
makeup	화장	hwa jang
male	남성	nam seong
man	남자	nam ja
manager	관리 책임자	gwal li chae gim ja
mango	망고	mang go
manicure	손톱 손질	son top son jil
many, much	많다, 많은	man ta, ma neun
map	지도	ji do

marble	대리석	dae ri seok
March	삼월	sa mwol
margarine	마아가린	ma a ga rin
marina (for yachts)	정박소	jeong bak so
marital status	결혼 여부	gyeol hon yeo bu
market	시장	si jang
married	결혼하다, 결혼한	gyeol hon ha da, gyeol hon han
massage, to	마사지하다	ma ssa ji ha da
mat (on floor)	깔개	kkal gae
mat (on table)	받침	bat chim
match, game	시합	si hap
matches	성냥	seong nyang
matte (photo)	매트지	mae teu ji
may	-아/어도 좋다	-a/eo do jo ta
May	오월	o wol
maybe	아마	a ma
mayonnaise	마요네즈	ma yo ne jeu
mayor	시장	si jang
meal	식사	sik sa
mean (word), to	의미하다	ui mi ha da
meaning	의미	ui mi
measure out, to	재다	jae da
measuring jug	계량컵	gye ryang keop
meat	고기	go gi
medicine	약	yak
meet, to	만나다	man na da
melon	참외	cha moe
member	회원	hoe won
member of parliament	국회의원	gu koe-ui won
membership card	회원권	hoe won kkwon
memory card	메모리 카드	me mo ri ka deu/ memory card
mend, to	고치다	go chi da
menstruation	생리	saeng ni
menu	메뉴	me nyu
message	메시지	me ssi ji
metal	금속	geum sok
meter (in taxi)	미터기	mi teo gi
metre	미터	mi teo
migraine	편두통	pyeon du tong
mild (taste)	순하다, 순한	sun ha da, sun han
milk	우유	u yu
millimeter	밀리미터	mil li mi teo
mind, be displeased, to	신경 쓰이다	sin-gyeong sseu i da
mine	내 것, 제 것	nae geot, je geot
mineral water	광천수	gwang cheon su
minute	분	bun
mirror	거울	geo.ul
miss (flight, train), to	놓치다	no chi da
miss (loved one), to	보고싶다, 보고싶어하다	bo go sip da, bo go si peo ha da
missing	없어지다, 없어진	eop seo ji da, eop seo jin
mist	안개	an gae
mistake	실수	sil su
mistaken	틀리다, 틀린	teul li da, teul lin
misty	뿌옇다, 뿌연	ppu yeo ta, ppu yeon

misunderstanding	오해	o hae
mixed	섞이다, 섞인	seo kki da, seo kkin
mobile phone	휴대전화	hyu dae jeon hwa
modern art	현대 미술	hyeon dae mi sul
moment (instant)	순간	sun-gan
Monday	월요일	wo ryo il
money	돈	don
monkey	원숭이	won sung-i
month	달	dal
moon	달	dal
moped	모터 자전거	mo teo ja jeon geo
more (comparative)	더	deo
morning	아침	a chim
mosquito	모기	mo gi
mosquito net	모기장	mo gi jang
most (superlative)	가장	ga jang
motel	모텔	mo tel
mother	어머니	eo meo ni
mother-in-law	시어머니, 장모	si eo meo ni, jang mo
motorbike	오토바이	o to ba i
motorboat	모터 보트	mo teo bo teu
mountain	산	san
mountain hut	산장	san jang
mouse (animal)	생쥐	saeng jwi
moustache	콧수염	ko ssu yeom
mouth	입	ip
movie	영화	yeong hwa
mp3 player	mp3 플레이어	em pi sseu ri peul le i eo/ mp3 player
MSG	조미료	jo mi ryo
much, many	많다, 많은	man ta, ma neun
mud	진흙	jin heuk
muscle	근육	geu nyuk
muscle spasms	근육 경련	geu nyuk gyeong nyeon
museum	박물관	bang mul gwan
mushroom	버섯	beo seot
music	음악	eu mak
must	-아/어야 하다	-a/eo ya ha da
my	내, 제	nae, je

N

nail (finger, toe)	손톱, 발톱	son top, bal top
nail (spike)	못	mot
nail file	손톱 줄	son top jul
nail scissors	손톱 가위	son top ga wi
naked	벌거벗다/-벗은	beol geo beot da/ -beo seun
name	이름	i reum
nappy, diaper	기저귀	gi jeo.gwi
nationality	국적	guk jeok
natural	자연(적인)	ja yeon(jeo gin)
nature	자연	ja yeon
nauseous	메스껍다, 메스꺼운	me seu kkeop da, me seu kkeo un
near	가까이	ga kka i
nearby	가까이에	ga kka i e

necessary	필요하다, 필요한	pi ryo ha da, pi ryo han
neck	목	mok
necklace	목걸이	mok geo ri
necktie	넥타이	nek tai
need, to	필요하다	pi ryo ha da
needle	바늘	ba neul
negative (photo)	네가티브	ne ga ti beu
neighbor	이웃(사람)	i ut(sa ram)
nephew	조카	jo ka
never	결코...아니다/ -지 않다	gyeol ko ...a ni da/ -ji an ta
new	새롭다, 새(로운)	sae rop da, sae(ro un)
news	뉴스	nyu seu
news stand	신문 가판대	sin mun ga pan dae
newspaper	신문	sin mun
next (in line, sequence)	다음(의)	da.eum(ui)
next to	...옆에	...yeo pe
nice	멋지다, 멋진	meot ji da, meot jin
nice (pleasant)	기분 좋다, 기분 좋은	gi bun jo ta, gi bun jo.eun
niece	조카딸	jo ka ttal
night	밤	bam
night duty	야간 근무	ya gan geun mu
night clothes	잠옷	ja mot
nightclub	나이트 클럽	na i teu keu leop
nightdress	잠옷	ja mot
nipple (bottle)	젖꼭지	jeot kkok ji
no (answer)	아뇨	a nyo
no entry	진입금지	ji nip geum ji
no thank you	괜찮아요	gwaen cha na yo
no, not (with nouns)	...아니다	...a ni da
no, not (with verbs and adjectives)	안, -지 않다	an, -ji an ta
no-one	아무도 ...아니다/ -지 않다	a mu do ...an i da/ -ji an ta
noise	소음	so-eum
nonstop (flight)	직항	ji kang
noodles	국수	guk su
normal	정상적이다/-적인	jeong sang jeo gi da, jeong sang jeo gin
north	북쪽	buk jjok
nose	코	ko
nosebleed	코피	ko pi
notebook	노트, 공책	no teu, gong chaek
notebook computer	노트북 (컴퓨터)	no teu buk (computer)/ notebook computer
notepad	노트, 공책	no teu, gong chaek
notepaper	편지지	pyeon ji ji
nothing	아무것도 ...아니나	a mu geot do ...a ni da
November	십일월	si bi rwol
now	지금	ji geum
nowhere	어디에도 ...없다	eo di e do ...eop da
number	숫자, 번호	sut ja, beon ho
number plate	번호판	beo no pan
nurse	간호사	gan ho sa
nuts	밤, 호두	bam, ho du

O

o'clock	…시	…si
object, thing	물체, 사물	mul che, sa mul
occupation	직업	ji geop
October	시월	si wol
off (gone bad)	상하다	sang ha da
off (turned off)	꺼져 있다	kkeo jyeo it da
offer, suggest, to	제의하다	je-ui ha da
office	사무실	sa mu sil
often	자주	ja ju
oil	기름	gi reum
ointment	연고	yeon-go
okay	좋다, 괜찮다	jo ta, gwaen chan ta
old (of persons)	나이 많다/많은	nai man ta/ma neun
on (turned on)	켜져 있다	kyeo jyeo it da
on board	타고 있다	ta go it da
on foot	걸어서	geo reo seo
on the left	왼쪽에	oen jjo ge
on the right	오른쪽에	o reun jjo ge
on the way	오는/가는 길에	o neun/ga neun gi re
oncoming car	맞은편에 오는 차량	ma jeun pyeo ne o neun cha ryang
one-way ticket	편도표	pyeon do pyo
one-way traffic	일방통행	il bang tong haeng
onion	양파	yang pa
open	열리다, 열린	yeol li da, yeol lin
open, to	열다	yeol da
operate (surgeon), to	수술하다	su sul ha da
operator (telephone)	교환	gyo hwan
opposite (contrary)	반대(의)	ban dae(ui)
optician	안경사, 안경점	an gyeong sa, an gyeong jeom
or	또는	tto neun
orange (color)	오렌지색	o ren ji saek
orange (fruit)	오렌지	o ren ji
order (command)	주문	ju mun
order something, to	주문하다	ju mun ha da
other	다른	da reun
other side	다른 쪽	da reun jjok
our	우리(의)	u ri(ui)
outside	바깥(쪽)	ba kkat(jjok)
outside of	…의 바깥에	…ui ba kka te
over there	저기(로)	jeo gi(ro)
overcome, to	이겨내다	i gyeo nae da
overpass, flyover	고가도로	go ga do ro
overseas	해외(의)	hae.oe(ui)
overtake, to	추월하다	chu wol ha da
oyster	굴	gul

P

packed lunch	도시락	do si rak
page	페이지	pe i ji
pain	통증	tong jjeung
painful	아프다, 아픈	a peu da, a peun
painkiller	진통제	jin tong je
paint	페인트	pe in teu
painting	그림, 칠	geu rim, chil

pajamas	파자마	pa ja ma
palace	궁	gung
pan	냄비	naem bi
pane	창유리	chang yu ri
panties	팬티	paen ti
pants	바지	ba ji
pantyhose	팬티 스타킹	pan ti seu ta king
paper	종이	jong-i
parasol	파라솔	pa ra sol
parcel	소포	so po
pardon me?	뭐라고 하셨어요?	mwo ra go ha syeo sseo yo?
parents	부모	bu mo
park (car), to	주차하다	ju cha ha da
park, gardens	공원	gong-won
parking garage	차고	cha go
parking space	주차장	Ju cha Jang
parliament	국회	guk hoe
part (of machine)	부속	bu sok
partner (in business)	동업자	dong-eop ja
partner (spouse)	배우자	bae-u ja
party (event)	파티	pa ti
passenger	승객	seung gaek
passport	여권	yeo kkwon
passport photo	여권 사진	yeo kkwon sa Jin
password	비밀번호, 암호	bi mil beon ho/am ho
patient (calm)	인내심 있다/-있는	in nae si mit da/-in neun
patient (doctor's)	환자	hwan ja
pay (bill), to	지불하다	ji bul ha da
peach	복숭아	bok sung-a
peanut	땅콩	ttang kong
pearl	진주	jin ju
peas	완두콩	wan du kong
pedal	페달	pe dal
pedestrian crossing	건널목	geon neol mok
pedicure	발톱 손질	bal top son jil
pen	펜	pen
penalty	벌금	heol geum
pencil	연필	yeon pil
penis	(남성) 성기	(nam seong) seong gi
penknife	주머니 칼	ju meo ni kal
people	사람들	sa ram deul
pepper, black	후추	hu chu
pepper, chilli	고추	go chu
performance	공연	gong yeon
perfume	향수	hyang su
perhaps, maybe	아마	a ma
period (menstrual)	생리	saeng.ni
permit, allow, to	허락하나	heo rak ha da
person	사람	sa ram
personal	개인적이다, 개인적인	gae in jeo gi da, gae in jeo gin
pet animal	애완동물	ae wan dong mul
petrol	휘발유	hwi bal lyu
petrol station	주유소	ju yu so
pharmacy, drugstore	약국	yak guk
phone	전화	jeon hwa

phone, to	전화하다	jeon hwa ha da
phone booth	전화 박스	jeon hwa bak seu
phone card	전화 카드	jeon hwa ka deu
phone directory	전화 번호부	jeon hwa beon ho bu
phone number	전화 번호	jeon hwa beon ho
photo (digital)	(디지털) 사진	(di ji teol) sa jin/(digital) sa jin
photocopier	복사기	bok sa gi
photocopy	복사	bok sa
photocopy, to	복사하다	bok sa ha da
photograph	사진	sa jin
photograph, to	사진 찍다	sa jin jjik da
phrasebook	숙어집	su geo jip
pick up (someone), to	태워주다	tae wo ju da
picnic	야유회	ya yu hoe
pillow	베개	be gae
pillowcase	베갯잇	be gaen nit
pills, tablets	알약	al lyak
pin	핀	pin
pineapple	파인애플	pa i nae peul
pipe (plumbing)	파이프	pa i peu
pipe (smoking)	파이프	pa i peu
pipe tobacco	파이프 담배	pa i peu dam bae
place of interest	관광 명소	gwan-gwang myeong so
plain (not flavored)	담백하다/-한	dam baek ha da, dam bae kan
plain (simple)	단순하다, 단순한	dan sun ha da, dan sun han
plan	계획	gye hoek
plane	비행기	bi haeng gi
plant	식물	sing mul
plastic	플라스틱	peul la seu tik
plastic bag	비닐 봉지	bi nil bong ji
plate	접시	jeop si
platform	플랫포옴	peul laet pom
play (drama)	연극	yeon-geuk
play (fun), to	놀다	nol da
play golf	골프 치다	gol peu chi da
play sports	운동 경기하다	un dong gyeong gi ha da
play tennis	테니스 치다	te ni seu chi da
playground	운동장	un dong jang
playing cards	카아드 놀이	kadeu no ri
pleasant	기분 좋다/좋은	gi bun jo ta/jo-eun
please (request)	좀 -어/아 주세요	jom -eo/a ju se yo
pleasure	기쁨	gi ppeum
plug (electric)	플러그	peul leo geu
plum	자두	ja du
pocket	호주머니	ho ju meo ni
pocketknife	주머니 칼	ju meo ni kal
point out, to	지적하다	ji jeok ha da
poison	독(약)	dok(yak)
poisonous	독이 있다/있는	do gi it da/in neun
police	경찰	gyeong chal
police officer	경찰관	gyeong chal gwan
police station	경찰서	gyeong chal seo
pond	연못	yeon mot
pony	조랑말	jo rang mal

pop music	대중음악	dae jung eu mak
population	인구	in.gu
pork	돼지고기	dwae ji go gi
port	항구	hang gu
porter (concierge)	수위	su wi
porter (for bags)	포터	po teo
possible	가능하다, 가능한	ga neung ha da, ga neung han
post office	우체국	u che guk
post, mail, to	부치다	bu chi da
postage	우편 요금	u pyeon yo geum
postage stamp	우표	u pyo
postbox	우체통	u che tong
postcard	엽서	yeop seo
post code	우편 번호	u pyeon beon ho
postpone, to	연기하다	yeon-gi ha da
potato	감자	gam ja
potato chips	감자 튀김	gam ja twi gim
powdered milk	분유	bu nyu
power outlet	콘센트	kon sen teu
prawn	새우	sae-u
precious metal	귀금속	gwi geum sok
precious stone	보석	bo seok
prefer, to	선호하다	seon ho ha da
preference	선호	seon ho
pregnant	임신하다, 임신한	im sin ha da, im sin han
prescription	처방(전)	cheo bang(jeon)
present (gift)	선물	seon mul
present (here)	출석하나, 출석한	chul seok ha da, chul seo kan
press, journalism	언론	eol lon
pressure	압력	am nyeok
price	가격	ga gyeok
price list	가격표	ga gyeok pyo
print (photo)	인화	in hwa
print, to	인화하다	in hwa ha da
probably	아마	a ma
problem	문제	mun je
profession	직업	jik geop
profit	이익	i ik
program, schedule	프로그램	peu ro geu raem
pronounce, to	발음하다	ba reum ha da
propane	프로판 가스	peu ro pan ga seu
pudding	푸딩	pu ding
pull a muscle	근육 이완	geu nyuk i wan
pull, to	당기다	dang gi da
pulse	맥박	maek bak
pure	순수하다, 순수한	sun su ha da, sun su han
purple	자주색	ja ju saek
purse (for money)	지갑	ji gap
push, to	밀다	mil da
puzzled	어리둥절하다/ -해하다	eo ri dung jeol ha da/ -hae ha da
pyjamas	파자마	pa ja ma

Q

quarter	4 분의 1	sa bu nui il

quarter of an hour	십오분	sip-o bun
queen	여왕	yeo wang
question	질문, 문제	jil mun, mun je
quick	빠르다, 빠른	ppa reu da, ppa reun
quiet	조용하다, 조용한	jo yong ha da, jo yong han

R

radio	라디오	ra di o
railroad, railway	철도	cheol tto
rain	비	bi
rain, to	비가 오다	bi ga o da
raincoat	비옷	bi ot
rape	강간	gang gan
rash	발진	bal jin
rat	쥐	jwi
rate of exchange (for foreign currency)	환율	hwan nyul
rate, tariff	요금	yo geum
raw, uncooked	날 (것의)	nal (geo sui)
razor blade	면도날	myeon do nal
read, to	읽다	il tta
really (in fact)	실제로	sil jje ro
really?	정말요?	jeong ma ryo?
reason	이유	i yu
receipt	영수증	yeong su jeung
receive, to	받다	bat da
reception desk	안내	an nae
recipe	조리법	jo ri beop
recommend, to	추천하다	chu cheon ha da
rectangle	직사각형	jik sa gak hyeong
red	빨갛다, 빨간	ppal ga ta, ppal gan
red wine	적포도주	jeok po do ju
reduction	축소	chuk so
refrigerator	냉장고	naeng jang go
refund	환불	hwan bul
region	지역, 지방	ji yeok, ji bang
registered	등록되다, 등록된	deung nok doe da, deung nok doen
relatives, family	친척	chin cheok
reliable	믿을 만하다, 믿을 만한	mi deul man ha da, mi deul man han
religion	종교	jong gyo
remains (historical)	유물	yu mul
rent out, to	세주다	se ju da
rent, to	임대하다	im dae ha da
repair, to	고치다	go chi da
repeat, to	반복하다	ban bok ha da
report (police)	보고서	bo go seo
reservation	예약	ye yak
reserve (ask for in advance), to	예약하다	ye yak ha da
responsible, to be	책임 있다/있는	chae gim it da/in neun
rest, relax, to	쉬다	swi da
restaurant	식당	sik dang
restroom	화장실	hwa jang sil
result	결과	gyeol gwa
retired	퇴직하다, 퇴직한	toe jik ha da, toe ji kan

return ticket	왕복표	wang bok pyo
reverse (car), to	뒤로 가다	dwi ro ga da
rheumatism	류머티즘	ryu meo ti jeum
ribbon	리본	ri bon
rice (cooked)	밥	bap
rice (grain)	쌀	ssal
rice (plant)	벼	byeo
ride, to	타다	ta da
ridiculous	어리석다, 어리석은	eo ri seok da, eo ri seo geun
riding (horseback)	말타기	mal ta gi
right of way	지금 당장	ji geum dang jang
right, correct	옳다, 옳은	ol ta, o reun
right-hand side	오른쪽	o reun jjok
rinse	헹굼	heng gum
ripe, to	익다, 익은	ik da, i geun
risk	위험	wi heom
river	강	gang
road	도로	do ro
roadway	차도	cha do
roasted, grilled, toasted	구운	gu un
rock (stone)	바위	ba wi
roll (bread)	롤빵	rol ppang
roof	지붕	ji bung
room	방, 룸	bang, rum
room number	룸 넘버	rum neon beo
room service	룸 서비스	rum seo bi seu
rope	밧줄	bat jul
route	루트	ru teu
rowing boat	나룻배	na rut bae
rubber	고무	go mu
rude	무례하다, 무례한	mu rye ha da, mu rye han
ruins	유적	yu jeok
run, to	달리다	dal li da
running shoes	조깅화	jo ging hwa

S

sad	슬프다, 슬픈	seul peu da, seul peun
safe	안전하다, 안전한	an jeon ha da, an jeon han
safe (for cash)	금고	geum go
safety pin	안전핀	an jeon pin
sail, to	항해하다	hang hae ha da
sailing boat	요트	yo teu
salad	샐러드	sael leo deu
sale (reduced prices)	세일	se il
sales clerk	점원	jeom won
salt	소금	so geum
salty	싸다, 싼	jja da, jjan
same	같다, 같은	gat da, ga teun
sandals	샌달	saen dal
sandy beach	백사장	baek sa jang
sanitary towel, sanitary napkin	생리대	saeng ni dae
satisfied	만족하다/-해하다	man jok ha da, man jo kae ha da
Saturday	토요일	to yo il

sauce	소스, 양념	so seu, yang nyeom
saucepan	냄비	naem bi
sauna	사우나	sa u na
save, keep, to	보관하다	bo gwan ha da
say, to	말하다	mal ha da
scald (injury)	물화상	mul hwa sang
scales	저울	jeo.ul
scan, to	스캔하다	seu kaen ha da/ scan-ha da
scarf	스카프	seu ka peu
scenic walk	전망이 좋은 산책로	jeon mang-i jo eun san chaeng no
school	학교	hak gyo
scissors	가위	g awi
Scotland	스코틀랜드	seu ko teul laen deu
screw	나사	na sa
screwdriver	드라이버	deu ra i beo
scuba diving	스쿠버 다이빙	seu ku beo da i bing
sculpture	조각	jo gak
sea	바다	ba da
seafood	해물	hae mul
seasick	배멀미	bae meol mi
seat	자리	ja ri
second (in line)	두 번째	du beon jjae
second (instant), in a	금방	geum bang
second-hand	중고	jung go
sedative	진정제	jin jeong je
see, to	보다	bo da
send, to	보내다	bon ae da
sentence	문장	mun jang
separate	각각(의)	gak gak(ui)
September	구월	gu wol
serious	심각하다, 심각한	sim gak ha da, sim ga kan
service	서비스	seo bi seu
service station	주유소	ju yu so
serviette, table napkin	냅킨	naep kin
sesame oil	참기름	cham gi reum
sesame seeds	참깨	cham kkae
set	세트	se teu
sew, to	바느질하다	ba neu jil ha da
shade	그늘	geu neul
shame, disgrace	수치	su chi
shampoo	샴푸	syam pu
shark	상어	sang-eo
shave, to	면도하다	myeon do ha da
shaver	면도기	myeon do gi
shaving cream	면도 크림	myeon do keu rim
she	그 여자	geu yeo ja
sheet (for bed)	시트	si teu
shirt	셔츠	syeo cheu
shoe polish	구두약	gu du yak
shoes	신발	sin bal
shop assistant	점원	jeo mwon
shop window	쇼 윈도우	syo win do u
shop, go shopping, to	쇼핑하다	syo ping ha da
shop, store	가게	ga ge

shopping center	쇼핑 센터	syo ping sen teo
short (not tall)	작다, 작은	jak da, ja geun
short circuit	합선	hap seon
shorts (short trousers)	반바지	ban ba ji
shorts (underpants)	팬티	paen ti
shoulder	어깨	eo kkae
show (live performance)	쇼	syo
show, to	보여주다	bo yeo ju da
shower, to take a	샤워하다	sya wo ha da
shrimp, prawn	새우	sae-u
shutter (camera)	셔터	seo teo
shutter (on window)	셔터	seo teo
sick, ill	아프다, 아픈	a peu da, a peun
sieve	체	che
sightseeing	시내 관광	si nae gwan-gwang
sign (road)	도로 표지	do ro pyo ji
sign, symbol	표시	pyo si
sign, to	서명하다	seo myeong ha da
signature	서명, 사인	seo myeong, ssa in
silent	고요하다, 고요한	go yo ha da, go yo han
silk	실크	sil keu
silver	은	eun
similar	비슷하다, 비슷한	bi seut ha da, bi seu tan
simple (easy)	쉽다, 쉬운	swip da, swi un
simple (uncomplicated)	간단하나/-한	gan dan ha da, gan dan han

sing, to	노래하다	no rae ha da
single (only one)	단 하나(의)	dan ha na(ui)
single (unmarried)	독신(의)	dok sin(ui)
single ticket	편도표	pyeon do pyo
sir (term of address)	…님	…nim
sister	자매	ja mae
sit down, to	앉다	an da
size	사이즈	sa i jeu
skiing	스키	seu ki
skin	피부	pi bu
skirt	치마	chi ma
Skype address	스카이프 수수	seu ka i peu ju so/ Skype ju so
sleep, to	자다	ja da
sleeping car	침대칸	chim dae kan
sleeping pills	수면제	su myeon je
sleeve	소매	so mae
slip (petticoat, underskirt)	슬립	seul lip
slippers	슬리퍼	seul li peo
slow	느리다, 느린	neu ri da, neu rin
slow train	완행 열차	wan haeng yeol cha
slowly	천천히	cheon cheon hi
small	작나, 작은	Jak da, Ja geun
small change	잔돈	jan don
smart phone	스마트폰	seu ma teu pon/smart phone
smell, bad odor	냄새	naem sae
smoke	연기	yeon-gi
smoke (tobacco), to	담배 피다	dam bae pi da
smoke detector	연기 경보기	yeon-gi gyeong bo gi
snake	뱀	baem

sneeze, to	재채기하다	jae chae gi ha da
snore, to	코 골다	ko gol da
snorkel	스노클링	seu no keul ling
snow	눈	nun
snow, to	눈이 오다	nu ni o da
soap	비누	bi nu
soap powder	세제	se je
soccer	축구	chuk gu
soccer match	축구 경기	chuk gu gyeong gi
socket (electric)	소케트	so ke teu
Social Media	소셜 미디어	so syeol mi di eo/Social Media
socks	양말	yang mal
soft drink	음료수	eum nyo su
software	소프트웨어	so peu teu we eo/software
sold out	매진	mae jin
sole (of shoe)	밑창	mit chang
somebody, someone	어떤 사람	eo tteon sa ram
something	어떤 것	eo tteon geot
sometimes	가끔	ga kkeum
somewhere	어딘가	eo din-ga
son	아들	a deul
soon	곧	got
sore throat	인후통	in hu tong
sore, painful	아프다, 아픈	a peu da, a peun
sorry!	미안합니다!	mi an ham ni da
soup (clear)	국	guk
soup (spicy stew)	찌개	jji gae
sour	시다, 신	si da, sin
south	남쪽	nam jjok
souvenir	기념품	gi nyeom pum
soy sauce	간장	gan jang
spanner, wrench	스패너	seu ppae neo
spare	스페어	seu ppe eo
spare parts	부품	bu pum
spare tyre	스페어 타이어	seu ppe o ta i eo
spare wheel	스페어 타이어	seu ppe o ta i eo
speak, to	말하다	mal ha da
specialist (doctor)	전문의	jeon mu nui
speciality (cooking)	특선 요리	teuk seon yo ri
speed	속도	sok do
speed limit	제한 속도	je han sok do
spell, to	철자하다	cheol jja ha da
spices	양념, 향료	yang nyeom, hyang nyo
spicy	맵다, 매운	maep da, mae.un
splinter	파편	pa pyeon
spoon	숟가락	su kka rak
sports	스포츠	seu po cheu
sports center	스포츠 센터	seu po cheu sen teo
spot (place)	지점	ji jeom
spot (stain)	점	jeom
spouse	배우자	bae-u ja
sprain	삠	ppim
spray	스프레이	seu peu re i
spring (device)	용수철	yong su cheol
spring (season)	봄	bom

square (plaza)	광장	gwang jang
square (shape)	정사각형	jeong sa gak hyeong
square meter	제곱 미터	je gop mi teo
squash (game)	스쿼시	seu kwo si
squid	오징어	o jing-eo
stadium	스타디움	seu ta di um
staff	직원	ji gwon
stain	얼룩	eol luk
stain remover	얼룩 제거제	eol luk je geo je
stairs	계단	gye dan
stamp (postage)	우표	u pyo
stand up, to	일어서다	i reo seo da
star	별	byeol
start, beginning	시작	si jak
start, to	시작하다	si jak ha da
station	역	yeok
stationery	문구	mun-gu
statue	동상	dong sang
stay overnight, to	묵다	muk da
stay, remain, to	머무르다	meo mu reu da
steal, to	훔치다	hum chi da
steamed	찌다, 찐	jji da, jjin
steel	강철	gang cheol
stepfather	계부	gye bu
stepmother	계모	gye mo
steps, stairs	계단	gye dan
sterilise, to	소독하다	so dok ha da
sticking plaster	반창고	ban chang go
sticky tape	테프	te peu
stitch (in wound), to	봉합하다	bong hap ha da
stomach (abdomen)	배	bae
stomach (organ)	위	wi
stomach ache	복통	bok tong
stomach cramps	위 경련	wi gyeong nyeon
stone	돌	dol
stools	대변	dae byeon
stop (bus)	정류장	jeong nyu jang
stop, cease	그만두다	geu man du da
stoop, halt to	멈추다	meom chu da
stopover	도중 하차	do jung ha cha
store, shop	가게	ga ge
storey (of a building)	...층 짜리	...cheung jja ri
storm	폭풍	pok pung
straight	똑바르다, 똑바른	ttok ba reu da, ttok ba reun
straight ahead	똑바로	ttok ba ro
straw (drinking)	스트로	seu teu ro
street	거리	geo ri
street vendor	자동 판매기	ja dong pan mae gi
strike (work stoppage)	파업	pa.eop
string	끈	kkeun
strong	힘세다, 힘센	him se da, him sen
student	학생	hak saeng
study (learn), to	공부하다	gong bu ha da
stuffed animal	동물 인형	dong mul in hyeong
subtitles	자막	ja mak
succeed, to	성공하다	seong gong ha da

sugar	설탕	seol tang
suit, business	정장	jeong jang
suitcase	여행가방	yeo haeng ga bang
summer	여름	yeo reum
sun	태양	tae yang
sunbathe	일광욕	il gwang yok
Sunday	일요일	i ryo il
sunglasses	선글라스	seon-geul las
sunlight	햇빛	haet bit
sunny	화창하다/-한	hwa chang ha da/-han
sunrise	일출	il chul
sunscreen	썬탠 크림	seon taen keu rim
sunset	일몰	il mol
sunshade	차일	cha il
sunstroke	일사병	il sa byeong
suntan lotion	썬탠 로션	seon taen ro syeon
suntan oil	썬탠 오일	seon taen oil
supermarket	수퍼마켓	supeo ma ket
surcharge	추가 요금	chu ga yo geum
surf	파도	pa do
surface mail	선편	seon yeon
surfboard	서핑 보드	seo ping bo deu
surname	성	seong
surprised	놀란	nol lan
swallow, to	삼키다	sam ki da
swamp	습지	seup ji
sweat	땀	ttam
sweat, to	땀 흘리다	ttam heul li da
sweater	스웨터	seu we teo
sweet	달다, 단	dal da, dan
sweetcorn	사탕 옥수수	sa tang ok su su
sweets, candy	사탕	sa tang
swim, to	수영하다	su yeong ha da
swimming costume, swimsuit	수영복	su yeong bok
swimming pool	수영장	su yeong jang
swindle	사기	sa gi
switch	스위치	seu wi chi
syrup	시럽	si reop

T

table	테이블	te i beul
table tennis	탁구	tak gu
tablecloth	테이블 보	te i beul ppo
table mat	접시 받침	jeop si bat chim
tablespoon	테이블 스푼	te i beul seu pun
tablets	알약	al lyak
tableware	식탁용구	sik ta kyong gu
take (medicine), to	(약을) 먹다	(yageul) meok da
take (photograph), to	(사진을) 찍다	(sa ji neul) jjik da
take (time), to	(시간이) 걸리다	(si ga ni) geol li da
take off (clothes), to	벗다	beot da
talk, to	말하다	mal ha da
tall	키 크다/큰	ki keu da/keun
tampon	탬폰	taem pon
tap	수도	su do
tap water	수돗물	su don mul
tape measure	줄자	jul ja

taste	맛	mat
taste, to	맛보다	mat bo da
tasty, delicious	맛있다, 맛있는	ma sit da, ma sin neun
tax	세금	se geum
tax-free shop	면세점	myeon se jeom
taxi	택시	taek si
taxi stand	택시 정류장	taek si jeong nyu jang
tea	차	cha
tea (green)	녹차	nok cha
tea cup	찻잔	chat jan
teapot	차 주전자	cha ju jeon ja
teaspoon	티 스푼	ti seu pun
teat (bottle)	젖병 꼭지	jeot byeong kkok ji
teeth	이	i
telephoto lens	망원 렌즈	mang.won len jeu
television	텔레비전	tel lebi jeon
telex	텔렉스	tel lek seu
tell, to	말히다	mal ha da
temperature (body)	체온	cheon
temperature (heat)	온도	on do
temple	절	jeol
temporary filling	임시 때움	im si ttae um
tender (sore)	무르다 무른	mu reu da, mu reun
tennis	데니스	te ni seu
tent	텐트	ten teu
terminus	종점	jong jeom
terrace	테라스	te ra seu
terribly	몹시	mop si
test	시험	si heom
text message	문자 (메시지)	mun ja (me si ji)/mun ja (message)
thank you! thanks!	감사합니다!	gam sa ham ni da!
thaw, to	녹이다	no gi da
theater (drama)	극장	geuk jang
theft	도난	do nan
there	저기에, 거기에	jeo gi e, geo gi e
thermometer (body)	체온계	cheon gye
thermometer (weather)	온도계	on do gye
they	그들	geu deul
thick (of liquids)	진하디, 진한	jin ha da, jin han
thick (of things)	두껍디, 두꺼운	du kkeop da, du kkeo.un
thief	도둑	do duk
thigh	허벅지	heo beok ji
thin (not fat)	마른	ma reun
thin (not thick)	묽은	mul geun
thing	물건	mul geon
think, have an opinion, to	생각하다	saeng gak ha da
think, ponder, to	숙고하다	suk go ha da
third	세 번째	se beon jjae
third(1/3), one third	삼분의 일	sam bu ne il
thirsty	목마르다, 목마른	mong ma reu da, mong ma reun
this afternoon	오늘 오후	o neul ohu
this evening	오늘 저녁	o neul jeo nyeok
this morning	오늘 아침	o neul a chim
thread	실	sil
throat	목(구멍)	mok(gu meong)

throat lozenges	기침 사탕	gi chim sa tang
thunderstorm	천둥 폭풍우	cheon dung pok pung-u
Thursday	목요일	mo gyo il
ticket	표	pyo
ticket office	매표소	mae pyo so
tidy	단정하다, 단정한	dan jeong ha da, dan jeong han
tie (necktie)	넥타이	nek ta i
tie, to	매다	mae da
tights, pantyhose	타이즈	ta i jeu
time (occasion)	시간	si gan
times (multiplying)	…배	…bae
timetable	시간표	si gan pyo
tin (can)	깡통	kkang tong
tin opener	깡통 따개	kkang tong tta gae
tip (gratuity)	팁	tip
tissues	티슈	ti syu
tobacco	담배	dam bae
today	오늘	o neul
toddler	유아	yu a
toe	발가락	bal kka rak
together	함께	ham kke
toilet	화장실	hwa jang sil
toilet paper	화장지	hwa jang ji
toilet seat	변기	byeon-gi
toiletries	세면 도구	se myeon do gu
tomato	토마토	to ma to
tomorrow	내일	nae-il
tongue	혀	hyeo
tonight	오늘밤	o neul ppam
tool, utensil, instrument	도구	do gu
tooth	이	i
toothache	치통	chi tong
toothbrush	칫솔	chi ssol
toothpaste	치약	chi yak
toothpick	이 쑤시개	i ssu si gae
top	꼭대기	kkok dae gi
top up, to	채우다	chae-u da
torch, flashlight	손전등	son jeon deung
total	합계	hap gye
tough	거칠다, 거친	geo chil da, geo chin
tour	투어	tu eo
tour guide	투어 가이드	tu eo ga i deu
tourist	관광객	gwan-gwang gaek
tourist class	투어 클라스	tu eo keul la s
tourist information office	관광 안내소	gwan-gwang an nae so
tow, to	끌다	kkeul da
tow cable	케이블	ke i beul
towel	수건	su geon
tower	탑	tap
town	마을, 시	ma-eul, si
town hall	구청	gu cheong
toy	장난감	jang nan kkam
traffic	교통	gyo tong
traffic light	신호등	sin ho deung
train	기차	gi cha
train station	역	yeok

train ticket	기차표	gi cha pyo
train timetable	기차 시간표	gi cha si gan pyo
translate, to	번역하다	beo nyeok ha da
travel agent	여행사	yeo haeng sa
travel, to	여행하다	yeo haeng ha da
traveler	여행자	yeo haeng ja
traveler's cheque	여행자 수표	yeo haeng ja su pyo
tree	나무	na mu
triangle	삼각형	sam gak hyeong
trim (haircut), to	(머리를) 다듬다	(meo ri reul) da deum da
trip, journey	여행	yeo haeng
trouble	문제	mun je
trousers	바지	ba ji
truck	트럭	teu reok
trust, to	믿다	mit da
trustworthy	믿을만한	mi deul man han
try on (clothes), to	입어보다	i beo bo da
try on (footwear), to	신어 보다	si neo bo da
try on (headgear), to	써보다	sseo bo da
tube (of paste)	튜브	tyu beu
Tuesday	화요일	hwa yo il
tuna	참치	cham chi
tunnel	터널	teo neol
turn off, to	끄다	kkeu da
turn on, to	켜다	kyeo da
turn over, to	뒤집다	dwi jip da
TV	티비	ti bi
TV guide	티비 방송안내	ti bi bang song an nae
tweet	트위더하다	teu wi teo ha da/ Tweeter-ha da
Tweeter	트위터	teu wi teo/Tweeter
tweezers	족집게	jok jip ge
twin-bedded	트윈 베드인	teu win be deu in
typhoon	태풍	tae pung
tyre	타이어	ta i eo
tyre pressure	타이어 압력	ta i eo am nyeok

U

ugly	못생기다, 못생긴	mot saeng gi da, mot saeng gin
ulcer	궤양	gwe yang
umbrella	우산	u san
under	…아래	…a rae
underpants	팬티	paen ti
underpass	지하도	ji ha do
understand, to	이해하다	i hae ha da
underwear	속옷	so got
undressed, to get	옷 벗다	ot beot da
unemployed	실직한	sil ji kan
uneven	고르지 않은	go reu ji a neun
United States	미국	mi guk
university	대학	dae hak
unleaded	무연	mu yeon
until	…까지, -(으)ㄹ 때까지	…kka ji, -(eu)l ttae kka ji
up, upward	…위에, …위로	…wi e, …wi ro
upright	똑바른, 똑바로	ttok ba reun, ttok ba ro

urgent	긴급한	gin-geu pan
urgently	긴급하게	gin.geu pa ge
urine	소변	so byeon
USB flash drive	USB (메모리 카드)	yu e seu bi (me mo ri ka deu)/USB (memory card)
use, to	사용하다	sa yong ha da
usually	보통	bo tong

V

vacate, to	비우다	bi u da
vacation	방학	bang hak
vaccination	예방 접종	ye bang jeop jong
vagina	(여성) 성기	(yeo seong) seong gi
valid	유효하다, 유효한	yu hyo ha da, yu hyo han
valley	계곡	gye gok
valuable	귀중하다, 귀중한	gwi jung ha da, gwi jung han
valuables	귀중품	gwi jung pum
van	봉고차	bong goc ha
vase	꽃병	kkot byeong
vegetables	야채	ya chae
vegetarian	채식주의자	chae sik ju-ui ja
vein	정맥	jeong maek
velvet	벨벳	bel bet
vending machine	자동 판매기	ja dong pan mae gi
venomous	독이 있다, 독이 있는	do gi it da, do gi in neun
venereal disease	성병	seong ppyeong
vertical	수직이다, 수직(인)	su ji gi da, su jig(in)
very	아주	a ju
vest, undershirt	조끼	jo kki
via	...을/를 거쳐서	...eul/reul geo chyeo seo
video camera	비디오 카메라	bi di o ka me ra
video cassette	비디오 (테이프)	bi di o (te i peu)
video recorder	비디오 (레코드)	bi di o (re ko deu)
view, look at, to	보다	bo da
view, panorama	경치	gyeong chi
village	마을	ma-eul
vinegar	식초	sik cho
visa	비자	bi ja
visit	방문	bang mun
visit, to pay a	방문하다	bang mun ha da
visiting time	방문 시간	bang mun si gan
visual (virtual) conference	화상 회의	hwa sang hoe ui
vitamin tablets	비타민(제)	bi ta min(je)
vitamins	비타민	bi ta min
volcano	화산	hwa san
volleyball	배구	bae gu
vomit, to	토하다	to ha da

W

wait for, to	기다리다	gi da ri da
waiter	종업원	jong eo bwon
waiting room	대기실	dae gi sil
waitress	종업원	jong-eo bwon
wake someone up, to	깨우다	kkae-u da
wake up, to	깨어나다	kkae-eo na da

walk (noun)	걷기	geot gi
walk, to	걷다	geot da
walking stick	지팡이	ji pang-i
wall	벽	byeok
wallet	지갑	ji gap
want, to	...을/를 원하다, -고 싶다	...eul/reul won ha da, -go sip da
wardrobe	옷장	ot jang
warn, to	경고하다	gyeong go ha da
warning	경고	gyeong go
wash, to	씻다	ssit da
washing	세탁	se tak
washing machine	세탁기	se tak gi
wasp	벌	beol
watch (wristwatch)	(손목)시계	(son mok)si gye
watch, look, see, to	보다	bo da
water	물	mul
water-skiing	수상 스키	su sang seu ki
waterfall	폭포	pok po
watermelon	수박	su bak
waterproof	방수	bang su
way (direction)	쪽	jjok
way (method)	방법	bang beop
way in	입구	ip gu
way out	출구	chul gu
we, us	우리	u ri
weak	약하다, 약한	yak ha da, ya kan
wear, to	입다	ip da
weather	날씨	nal ssi
weather forecast	일기예보	il gi ye bo
wedding	결혼식	gyeol hon sik
Wednesday	수요일	su yo il
week	주	ju
weekday	주중	ju jung
weekend	주말	ju mal
weigh, to	...의 무게를 달다	...ui mu ge reul dal da
weigh out, to	달아내다	da ra nae da
welcome!	어서 오세요!	eo seo o se yo!
well (for water)	우물	u mul
well (good)	잘	jal
west	서쪽	seo jjok
westerner	서양 사람	seo yang sa ram
wet	젖다, 젖은	jeot da, jeo jeun
what?	뭐라고요?	mwo ra go yo?
wheel	바퀴	ba kwi
wheelchair	휠체어	hwil che eo
when?	언제요?	eon je yo?
whenever	-(으)ㄹ 때마다	-(eu)l ttae ma da
where to?	어디로 가세요?	eo di ro ga se yo?
where?	어디요?	eo di yo?
which?	어느 거요?	eo neu geo yo?
white	하얗다, 하얀	ha ya ta, ha yan
white wine	백포도주	baek po do ju
who?	누구요?	nu gu yo?
why?	왜요?	wae yo?
widow	과부	gwa bu
widower	홀아비	ho ra bi

wife	아내	a nae
wind, breeze	바람	ba ram
window (for paying, buying tickets)	창구	chang gu
window (in house)	창문	chang mun
windscreen wiper	와이퍼	wa i peo
windscreen, windshield	(자동차) 앞유리	(ja dong cha) am nyu ri
wine	포도주	po do ju
winter	겨울	gyeo-ul
wire	철사	cheol ssa
wireless connection	무선 인터넷	mu seon in teo net/ mu seon Internet
wish, to	바라다	ba ra da
witness	목격자	mok gyeok ja
woman	여자	yeo ja
wonderful	멋지다, 멋진	meot ji da, meot jin
wood	나무	na mu
wool	울, 양모	ul, yang mo
word	단어	da neo
work, occupation	일, 직업	il, ji geop
work, to	일하다	il ha da
working day	근무일	geun mu il
worn out (clothes)	닳아버리다/-버린	da ra beo ri da, da ra beo rin
worn out, tired	피곤하다, 피곤한	pi gon ha da, pi gon han
worry, to	걱정하다	geok jeong ha da
wound	상처	sang cheo
wrap, to	싸다	ssa da
wrench, spanner	스패너	seu pae neo
wrist	손목	son mok
write down	적다	jeok da
write, to	쓰다	sseu da
writing pad	공책	gong chaek
writing paper	편지지	pyeon ji ji
wrong (mistaken)	틀리다, 틀린	teul li da, teul lin

Y

yawn	하품	ha pum
year	년	nyeon
years old	…살, …세	…sal, …se
yellow	노랗다, 노란	no ra ta, no ran
yes	네, 예	ne, ye
yes please	네, 그렇게 해 주세요.	ne, geu reo ke hae ju se yo
yesterday	어제	eo je
you (audience)	여러분	yeo reo bun
you (familiar)	너, 너희(들)	neo, neo hui(deul)
you (female)	아가씨, 아주머니	a ga ssi, a ju meo ni
you (male)	아저씨, 선생님	a jeo ssi, seon saeng nim
you're welcome (to thanks)	괜찮아요!	gwaen cha na yo!
youth hostel	유스 호스텔	yu seu ho seu tel

Z

zip (fastener)	지퍼	ji peo
zoo	동물원	dong mu rwon
zucchini	애호박	ae ho bak